ARMENIA	AUSTRALIA	AUSTRIA	AZERBAIJAN	BAHAMAS		DESH
NIA-HERZEGOVINA	BOTSWANA	BRAZIL	BRUNEI	BULGARIA		NDI
CHINA	COLOMBIA	COMOROS	CONGO	CONGO (DEM. REP.)	COSTA RICA	COTE D'IVOIRE
MINICAN REPUBLIC	ECUADOR	EGYPT	EL SALVADOR	EQUATORIAL GUINEA	ERITREA	ESTONIA
GEORGIA	GERMANY	GHANA	GREECE	GREENLAND	GRENADA	GUATEMALA
INDIA	INDONESIA	IRAN	IRAQ	IRELAND	ISRAEL	ITALY
KOREA, SOUTH	KOSOVO	KUWAIT	KYRGYZSTAN	LAOS	LATVIA	LEBANON
MADAGASCAR	MALAWI	MALAYSIA	MALDIVES	MALI	MALTA	MARSHALL ISLANDS
MOROCCO	MOZAMBIQUE	MYANMAR (BURMA)	NAMIBIA	NAURU	NEPAL	NETHERLANDS
PAKISTAN	PANAMA	PAPUA NEW GUINEA	PARAGUAY	PERU	PHILIPPINES	POLAND
O TOMÉ & PRÍNCIPE	SAUDI ARABIA	SENEGAL	SERBIA	SEYCHELLES	SIERRA LEONE	SINGAPORE
ST KITTS & NEVIS	ST LUCIA	ST VINCENT	SUDAN	SUDAN, SOUTH	SURINAME	SWEDEN
TOGO	TONGA	TRINIDAD & TOBAGO	TUNISIA	TURKEY	TURKMENISTAN	TUVALU
VANUATU	VATICAN CITY	VENEZUELA	VIETNAM	YEMEN	ZAMBIA	ZIMBABWE

GW00833033

TO RACHEL AND STEVEN

First published in Great Britain in 1987
by Philip's, a division of Octopus Publishing Group Limited
(www.octopusbooks.co.uk)
Carmelite House, 50 Victoria Embankment, London EC4Y 0DZ
An Hachette UK Company (www.hachette.co.uk)

Fifteenth edition 2019

Text © 1987, 2013, 2016, 2019 David and Jill Wright
Maps © 2019 Philip's

Cartography by Philip's

A CIP catalogue record for this book is available from the British Library.

ISBN 978–1–84907–491–9

All rights reserved. Apart from any fair dealing for the purpose of private
study, research, criticism or review, as permitted under the Copyright,
Designs and Patents Act, 1988, no part of this publication may be
reproduced, stored in a retrieval system, or transmitted in any form
or by any means, electronic, electrical, chemical, mechanical, optical,
photocopying, recording, or otherwise, without prior written permission.
All enquiries should be addressed to the Publisher.

Printed in Malaysia

Details of other Philip's titles and services can be found
on our website at: **www.philips-maps.co.uk**

PICTURE ACKNOWLEDGEMENTS

Alamy /Andalucia Plus Image bank 41 top, /Tom Bean 76 bottom, /blickwinkel 78 centre right, /Mark Boulton 67 top, /Jon Crwys-Williams 86 bottom centre, /Ian Dagnall 22 top, /Rick Dalton – Ag 76 centre left, /Danita Delimont 24 centre left, /Pavel Filatov 40 bottom right, /Gallo Images 42 bottom right, /Alan Gignoux 10 bottom, /Robert Harding Picture Library Ltd 58 bottom centre, 64 centre, /Robert Harding World Imagery 40 bottom centre, /Imagestate Media Partners Limited – Impact Photos 42 top, /Hideo Kurihara 64 top, /LOOK Die Bildagentur der Fotografen/GmbH 66 bottom right, 69, /Sabine Lubenow 24 bottom right, /Novarc Images 86 top, /Purepix 53 top, /Feije Riemersma 43 right, /Juergen Ritterbach 85, /Pep Roig 84 bottom centre, /Isidoro Ruiz/Iruizimages.com 19 right, /Kevin Shields 74 top, /Ashley Simmons 32 bottom, /Friedrich Stark 56 bottom centre, 46 bottom left, 88 left, /Johnny Stockshooter 34 bottom right, /tbkmedia.de 23, /vario images GmbH & Co.KG 28 centre right, /John Warburton-Lee Photography 59, /weberfoto 72 top; **Corbis** /Tiziana & Gianni Baldizzone 20 centre, /John Carnemolla 66 bottom left, /DLILLC 48 bottom left, /Kevin Fleming 49 left, /Free Agents Limited 20 top, /Jason Hawkes 22 bottom left, /Jason Hosking/zefa 50 bottom right, /Richard Hutchings 2, /Charles & Josette Lenars 11 left, /James Montgomery/JAI 50 bottom left, /Bruno Morandi/Robert Harding World Imagery 48 centre right, /Patrick Robert/Sygma 51, /Dietrich Rose/zefa 19 centre, /Bill Ross 74 left, /Royalty-Free 13, /Robin Utrecht Fotografie/HillCreek Pictures 83, /Tony Waltham/Robert Harding World Imagery 88 top, /Nik Wheeler 54 bottom right, 68, /Michael S. Yamashita 50 centre; **Dreamstime.com** /Blueice69c., /Dragoneye 45 top centre, /Nalukai 72 bottom; **Finnish Tourist Board** 20 bottom right; **Fotolia.com** /Gary 70 top, /Eric Gevaert 47, /Klaus Heidemann 80 bottom, /jelwolf 24 bottom centre, /Stefanos Kyriazis 35, /QiangBa DanZhen 48 bottom centre, /Zechal 36 bottom left; **Fugro/NPA Ltd** 5 bottom left, 5 bottom right, 33; **Getty Images** /VII-photo 48 bottom right; **Robert Harding Picture Library** 14, 30 centre right, 30 bottom, 34 bottom left, 36 centre right, 41 middle centre, 44 top, 46 top, 64 centre left, 64 centre right, 79, 80 top, 81 left, 82, /David Beatty 40 bottom left, /P. Bordes 56 top, /C. Bowman 32 centre left, 78 top, /Rob Cousins 26 centre, 46 bottom right, /Nigel Francis 26 centre left, /Simon Harris 77 top, /Kim Hart 19 left, /Gavin Hellier 77 bottom, /F. Jackson 12, /Thomas Laird 45 bottom, /Louise Murray 25, /Geoff Renner 89, /Christopher Rennie 84 bottom right, /Michael Short 34 top, /J. H. C. Wilson 45 top right; **James Hughes** 22 bottom right; **Hulton Deutsch Collection** 54 bottom left; **Hutchison Library** /Sarah Errington 58 top, /Tony Souter 30 centre left; **Image Bank** /Kaz Mori 75 top right, /Jeffrey M. Spielman 8, /Harald Sund 40 top, /Hans Wolf 28 top, 28 bottom left; **iStock** /06photo 48 top, /AndreaWillmore 60 bottom left, /BirdImages 72 centre right, /dan_prat 71, /DonFink 75 bottom right, /FrankRamspott 43, /hadynyah 58 centre right, /JeremyRichards 87 bottom, /Jillian Cooper 70 bottom left, /JLGutierrez 30 top, /millerpd 58 bottom right, /oversnap 52 top, /Sirimo 74 centre bottom, stefaniedesign 66 top, /tupatu76 86 centre right; **Nina Jenkins** 54 centre, 56 centre right; **NASA** 5 (planet insets); **Panos Pictures** /Gary John Norman 57 left; **Planet Earth Pictures** /John Eastcott 6; **Octopus Publishing Group Ltd** /Graham Kirk 78 bottom left, /Paul Williams 46 bottom centre; **Science Photo Library** /P. G. Adam, Publiphoto Diffusion 81 right, /European Space Agency 4, /John Mead 63; **Shutterstock** /dibrova right, /Nina Janesikova 62 top, /kropic1 right, /Tupungato 28 bottom right, /Vladimir Zhoga 50 centre right, **Still Pictures** /Chris Caldicott 54 top, /Mark Edwards 56 bottom left, 84 bottom left, /John Maier 10 top, 61, /Roland Seitre 62; **Thinkstock** 15 right, 22 centre left, 22 centre, 24 top, 24 centre right, 26 bottom centre, 28 bottom centre, 29, 30 centre, 32 top, 38, 39, 50 top, 55, 58 bottom left, 60 top, 66 bottom centre, 70 bottom left, 70 bottom right, 75 top left, 76 top, 77 top left, 84 top, 86 bottom left, 87 top; **Tony Stone Images** 60 bottom right, /Trevor Wood 44 left; **David & Jill Wright** 15 left, 16 bottom right, 18, 20 bottom left, 21, 26 top left, 26 top right, 37, 42 bottom left, 44 centre left, 52 bottom, 57 right, 60 bottom centre, 67 bottom.
Front cover: Horvath Zoltan/Dreamstime.com. left, prapass/Shutterstock centre, Fatseyeva/Shutterstock right.

Royal Geographical Society with IBG

Advancing geography and geographical learning

Philip's World Atlases are published in association with The Royal Geographical Society (with The Institute of British Geographers).

The Society was founded in 1830 and given a Royal Charter in 1859 for 'the advancement of geographical science'. Today it is a leading world centre for geographical learning – supporting education, teaching, research and expeditions, and promoting public understanding of the subject.

Further information about the Society and how to join may be found on its website at: www.rgs.org

PHILIP'S
Children's
ATLAS

DAVID AND JILL WRIGHT

IN ASSOCIATION WITH
THE ROYAL GEOGRAPHICAL SOCIETY
WITH THE INSTITUTE OF BRITISH GEOGRAPHERS

**Royal
Geographical
Society**
with IBG

Advancing geography
and geographical learning

CONTENTS

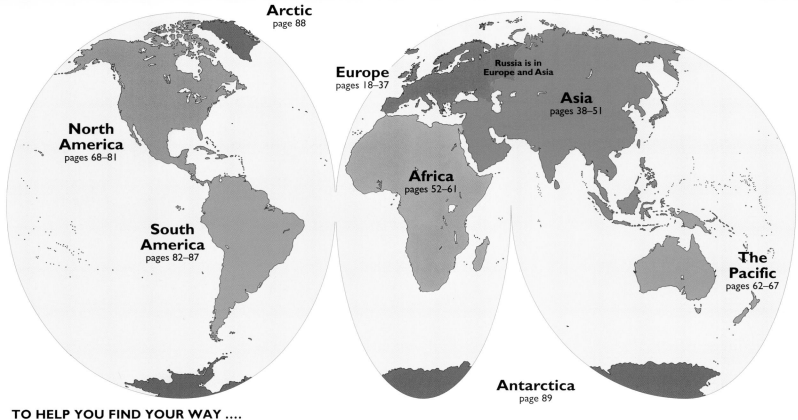

Arctic
page 88

Europe
pages 18–37

Asia
pages 38–51

Russia is in Europe and Asia

North America
pages 68–81

Africa
pages 52–61

South America
pages 82–87

The Pacific
pages 62–67

Antarctica
page 89

TO HELP YOU FIND YOUR WAY ....
Each continent is COLOUR-CODED on this map
AND on the contents page (opposite) AND on the heading of each atlas page.

ABOUT THIS ATLAS

Philip's Children's Atlas is written by people who enjoy learning about our wonderful world and want others to enjoy it, too. David and Jill Wright have taught geography in schools and colleges. We have visited more than a hundred countries to understand the scenery and people better and to take photographs. Some of these visits have been made with our own children or with student groups. This has helped us to see the world through children's eyes.

There is so much we want to tell you about, and so little space. We have had to choose what to write about and what to leave out – very hard! The world is always changing too, and this new edition has the very latest facts and figures. So we hope this atlas will help YOU, the reader, to begin a lifelong exploration of the world, to notice all the links we have with all parts of the world, and to find out more from other books and websites.

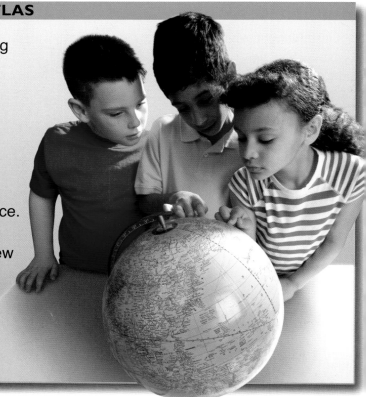

OUR PLANET EARTH

Our Planet Earth	4–5
Mountains, Plains and Seas	6–7
The Countries of the World	8–9
People of the World	10–11
Cold and Hot Lands	12–13
Wet and Dry Lands	14–15
Enjoying Maps	16–17

EUROPE

Europe	18–19
Scandinavia	20–21
The UK and Ireland	22–23
Benelux	24–25
France	26–27
Germany and Austria	28–29
Spain and Portugal	30–31
Switzerland and Italy	32–33
South-east Europe	34–35
Eastern Europe	36–37

ASIA

Asia	38–39
Russia and Neighbours	40–41
Middle East	42–43
South Asia	44–45
South-east Asia	46–47
China and Mongolia	48–49
Japan and Korea	50–51

AFRICA

Africa	52–53
North Africa	54–55
West Africa	56–57
Central and East Africa	58–59
Southern Africa	60–61

THE PACIFIC

The Pacific	62–63
Australia	64–65
New Zealand	66–67

NORTH AMERICA

North America	68–69
Canada	70–71
United States of America	72–73
Eastern USA	74–75
Western USA	76–77
Central America	78–79
West Indies	80–81

SOUTH AMERICA

South America	82–83
Tropical South America	84–85
Temperate South America	86–87

THE ARCTIC AND ANTARCTICA

The Arctic	88
Antarctica	89

QUIZ QUESTIONS AND INDEX

Quiz Questions	90–91	Glossary	96–97
Index	92–95	Answers to Questions	97

OUR PLANET EARTH

OUR Earth is made of layers of rock. The diagram below shows the Earth with a slice cut out. The hottest part is the core, at the centre. Around the core is the mantle, which is probably slightly liquid and moves very slowly. The outer layer, the crust, is quite thin under the oceans, but it is thicker under the continents.

Scientists now know that the Earth's crust is cracked, like the shell of a hard-boiled egg that has been dropped. The cracks are called faults. The huge sections of crust divided by the faults are called plates and they are moving very, very slowly. The continents have gradually moved across the Earth's surface as the crustal plates have moved. Sudden movements near the faults cause volcanic eruptions or earthquakes. Undersea earthquakes cause huge waves called tsunamis.

CRUST **MANTLE**

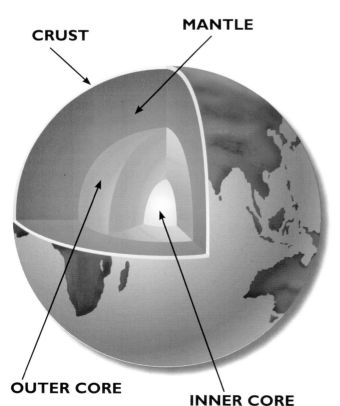

OUTER CORE **INNER CORE**

▲ *The Earth from space:* this satellite image shows Africa, Arabia, the Mediterranean Sea and Europe. The Sahara Desert has no cloud and is all sunny. Some of the white clouds near the Equator show where there are thunderstorms.
  Can you name the oceans to the west (left) and to the east (right) of Africa? And can you name the continent – and the country – on the far west (left) of this image? (The maps on pages 7 and 8 will help you. Answers on page 97.)

FASCINATING FACTS ABOUT THE EARTH

DISTANCE AROUND THE EQUATOR 40,075 kilometres
DISTANCE AROUND THE POLES 40,007 kilometres
DISTANCE TO THE CENTRE OF THE EARTH 6370 kilometres
SURFACE AREA OF THE EARTH 510,065,600 square kilometres
PROPORTIONS OF SEA AND LAND 71% sea; 29% land
DISTANCE FROM THE EARTH TO THE SUN 150,000,000 kilometres
  (It takes 8½ minutes for the Sun's light to reach the Earth.)
DISTANCE FROM THE EARTH TO THE MOON 384,400 kilometres
THE EARTH TRAVELS AROUND THE SUN at 107,000 kilometres per hour, or nearly 30 kilometres per second
THE EARTH'S ATMOSPHERE is about 175 kilometres high
CHIEF GASES IN THE ATMOSPHERE Nitrogen 78%; oxygen 21%
AVERAGE DEPTH OF SEA 3900 metres
AVERAGE HEIGHT OF LAND 880 metres

The Earth travels round the Sun in 365¼ days, which we call a year. Every four years we add an extra day to February to use up the ¼ days. This is called a Leap Year. The Earth travels at a speed of over 107,000 kilometres an hour. (You have travelled 600 kilometres through space while reading this!)

The Earth also spins round and round as it travels through space. It spins round once in 24 hours, which we call a day. Places on the Equator are spinning at 1660 kilometres an hour. Because of the way the Earth moves, we experience day and night, and different seasons during a year (see page 13). No part of our planet is too hot or too cold for life to survive. Yet the Earth is 150 million kilometres from the Sun.

The Moon is our nearest neighbour in space. It is 384,400 kilometres away. The first men to reach the Moon took four days to travel there in 1969. On the way, they took many photos of the Earth, such as the one on the left. The Earth looks very blue from space because of all the sea. It is the only planet in the Solar System with sea. Look at the swirls of cloud. These show that the Earth has an atmosphere. Our atmosphere contains oxygen and water vapour, and it keeps all living things alive.

The diagram below shows all the planets in our Solar System. The Earth is the third planet from the Sun.

THE SOLAR SYSTEM – RELATIVE SIZES OF THE PLANETS

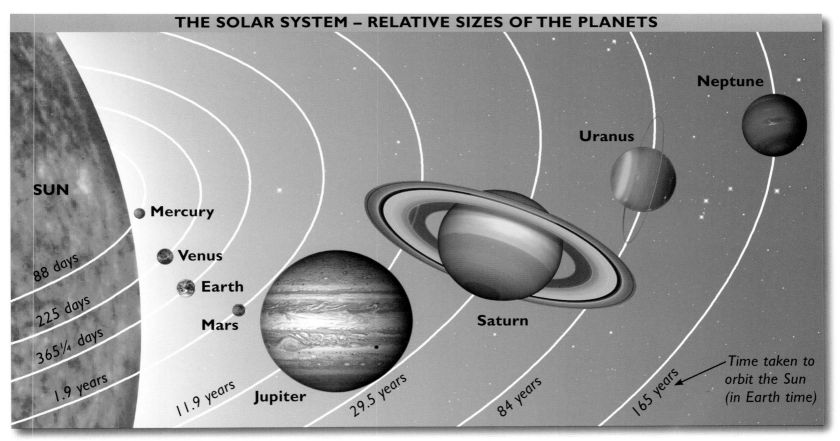

SUN

Mercury — 88 days

Venus — 225 days

Earth — 365¼ days

Mars — 1.9 years

Jupiter — 11.9 years

Saturn — 29.5 years

Uranus — 84 years

Neptune — 165 years

Time taken to orbit the Sun (in Earth time)

EARTH FROM SPACE

◄ *Glaciers in the Himalayas,* as can be seen from space. The white stripes are glaciers, or 'rivers of ice' in the valleys. There is snow on the mountains.

▶ *The Great Lakes* from space. Look at the map on page 75 to find their names. On the east (right) is the Atlantic Ocean.

MOUNTAINS, PLAINS AND SEAS

THE map shows that there is much more sea than land in the world. Over two-thirds of the Earth's surface is covered with water or ice. The Pacific is by far the biggest ocean; the map splits it in two.

The mountains are shown with shadows on this map. Look for the world's highest mountain range – the Himalayas, in Asia. There are high mountains on the western side of both American continents. Most of the world's great mountain ranges have been made by folding in the Earth's crust.

The green expanse across northern Europe and northern Asia is the world's biggest plain.

STANDARD POSTAGE
1998 NAMIBIA
T. Breckwoldt Namibian coast

▲ **The Atlantic Ocean** washes the desert shore of Namibia, in southern Africa.

MOUNTAINS AND PLAINS

In which country does this animal live? (**Answer on page 97.**)

▲ **Farming the Great Plains of North America.** The Plains cover large areas of the USA and Canada. This land in Alberta, Canada, has just been harvested. The almost flat land of the Great Plains ends where the Rocky Mountains begin.

To see all of **Antarctica** turn to page 89.

MOUNTAINS, PLAINS AND SEAS

WORLD RECORDS: LARGEST • LONGEST • HIGHEST • DEEPEST

LARGEST OCEAN Pacific, 155,557,000 sq km

DEEPEST PART OF OCEANS Mariana Trench, 11,022 metres (Pacific)

LARGEST LAKE Caspian Sea, 371,000 sq km (Europe and Asia)

DEEPEST LAKE Lake Baikal, 1620 metres (Russia)

LONGEST RIVERS Nile, 6695 km (Africa); Amazon, 6450 km (South America); Yangtze, 6380 km (Asia)

LARGEST ISLANDS Australia, 7,690,000 sq km; Greenland, 2,175,600 sq km

LARGEST DESERT Sahara, 9,100,000 sq km (Africa)

HIGHEST MOUNTAIN Everest, 8850 m (Asia)

LONGEST MOUNTAIN RANGE Andes, 7200 km (South America)

LONGEST GORGE Grand Canyon, 446 km (North America)

HIGHEST WATERFALL Angel Falls, 979 metres (Venezuela, South America)

Scale along the Equator 1:108 000 000

0   1000   2000   3000   4000 km

1 cm on the map = 1080 km on the ground

0   1000   2000 miles

1 inch on the map = 1705 miles on the ground

Height of the land

▲ High mountains
▼ Deep sea trenches

over 6000 metres
4000 – 6000
2000 – 4000
1000 – 2000
400 – 1000
200 – 400
0 – 200 metres
sea level
below sea level

THE COUNTRIES OF THE WORLD

A D-I-Y QUIZ

On this map, some small countries are labelled with only the first few letters of their name. Try to guess the whole name. Then check your answers on the continent maps: *Europe page 19; Asia page 39; Africa page 53; Pacific pages 62–63; West Indies page 81; South America page 83.*

FIVE of the continents of the world are divided into countries.

Look at the borders between countries: they have all been decided by people. Some follow natural features, such as rivers or mountain ranges. But some borders separate people of the same language, and this can cause problems.

This map has been drawn to show each country at the correct size. So you can see which countries are big, which are middle-sized and which are small. But because the sizes are correct, some of the shapes are not quite right. To see **both** correct size **and** correct shape we all need to look at a globe.

▲ **The United Nations flag** with an unusual map of the world surrounded by olive branches for peace.

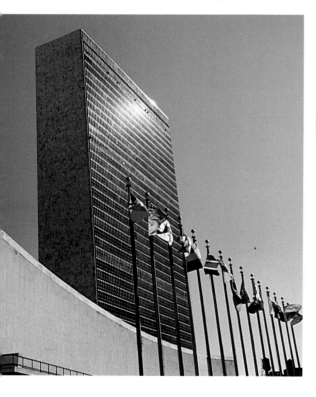

▲ **The United Nations building,** in New York City, USA. The world's problems are discussed here – and sometimes solved.

WHICH ARE THE WORLD'S BIGGEST COUNTRIES?

Only five of the 'top ten' countries with large populations are also among the 'top ten' biggest countries.

TOP TEN COUNTRIES BY SIZE (SQUARE KILOMETRES)				TOP TEN COUNTRIES BY POPULATION			
1. Russia	17,075,400	6. Australia	7,741,220	1. China	1385 million	6. Pakistan	208 million
2. Canada	9,970,610	7. India	3,287,263	2. India	1297 million	7. Nigeria	203 million
3. USA	9,629,091	8. Argentina	2,780,400	3. USA	329 million	8. Bangladesh	159 million
4. China	9,596,961	9. Kazakhstan	2,724,900	4. Indonesia	263 million	9. Russia	142 million
5. Brazil	8,514,215	10. Algeria	2,381,741	5. Brazil	209 million	10. Japan	126 million

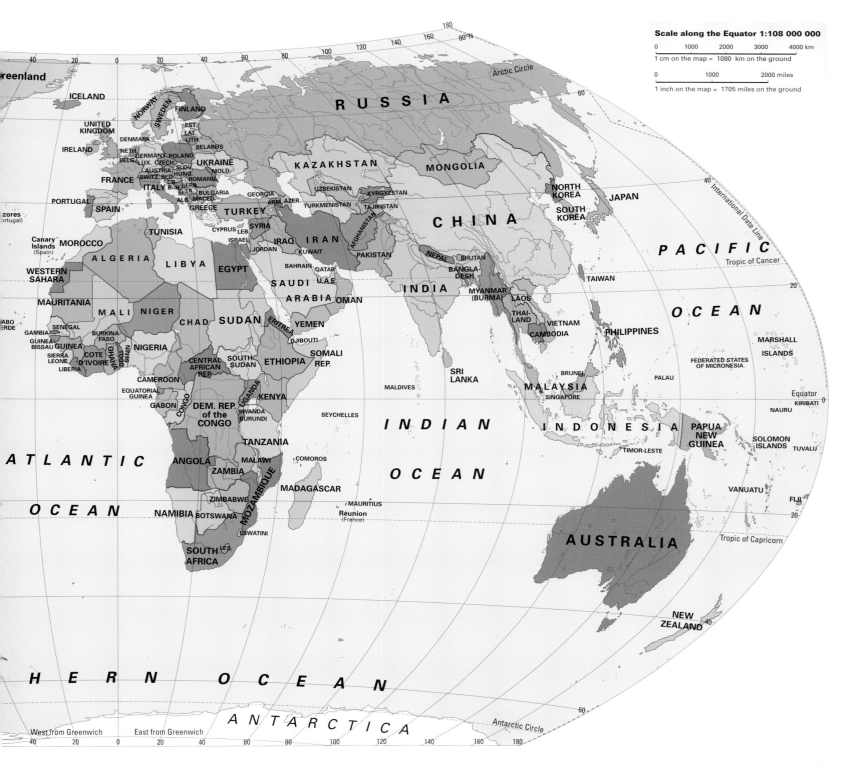

Scale along the Equator 1:108 000 000

0   1000   2000   3000   4000 km

1 cm on the map = 1080 km on the ground

0   1000   2000 miles

1 inch on the map = 1705 miles on the ground

PEOPLE OF THE WORLD

THERE is *one* race of people: the human race. In Latin, we are all known as *Homo sapiens* – 'wise person'. The differences between people, such as dark or light skin, hair and eyes, are small.

The smaller map (below) shows the rich and the poor countries of the world. In any one country there are rich and poor people, but the difference between countries is even greater.

The map shows that the richest countries are in North America, Europe, Japan and Australia. Here most people usually have plenty to eat. They can buy many kinds of food; they can go to a doctor or hospital when they need to, and the children can go to school.

The richest countries are the ones that control most of the world's trade and make decisions about international rules. But they also give aid to help the poorer countries.

The poorest countries (shown in dark green) are in the tropics – mostly in Africa. Life in these countries is very different from life in the rich world. Many people struggle to grow enough food, and they are often hungry.

People who do not have enough to eat find it difficult to work hard and they get ill more easily. They do not have enough money to pay for medicines or to send their children to school to learn to read and write. Some of the poorest people live in shanty towns in or near large cities.

But many people in the tropics do manage to break out of this 'cycle of poverty'. They now have a better diet, and more and more people can obtain clean water. Primary schools now teach most children to read and write and do simple arithmetic – though there are few books and classes may be very large. In many places, village health workers are taught to recognize and treat the common diseases.

▲ **Crowded and poor:** *a shanty town in Brazil. These shanties on a steep hillside in Rio de Janeiro were built by people who have nowhere else to live. Some of them have low-paid jobs, but others have to beg to get enough to eat.*

THIRD WORLD AID

This young boy is collecting water from a tap in his village in Uganda. Now he and his family have clean, safe water to drink and wash in. They no longer have to walk far for water. Many schemes like this are helped by money given by the rich countries of the world.

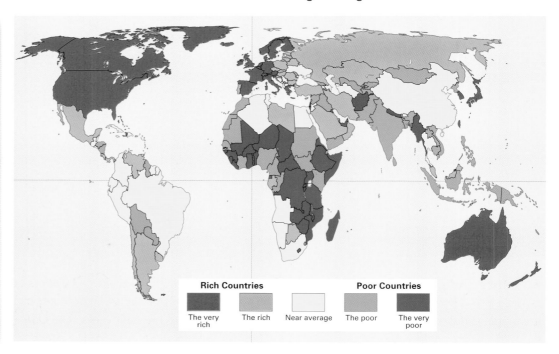

Rich Countries			Poor Countries	
The very rich	The rich	Near average	The poor	The very poor

The map below shows where the world's people live. The darker the colour, the more people there are. Most of the world has very few people: the cream or yellow areas.

The areas with few people are mostly desert, or high mountains, or dense forests, or very cold. Over half the world's people live in the lowlands of south and east Asia.

Other crowded areas are parts of Europe and the Nile Valley. The most crowded places of all are the big cities. Find the cities with more than 10 million people on the map.

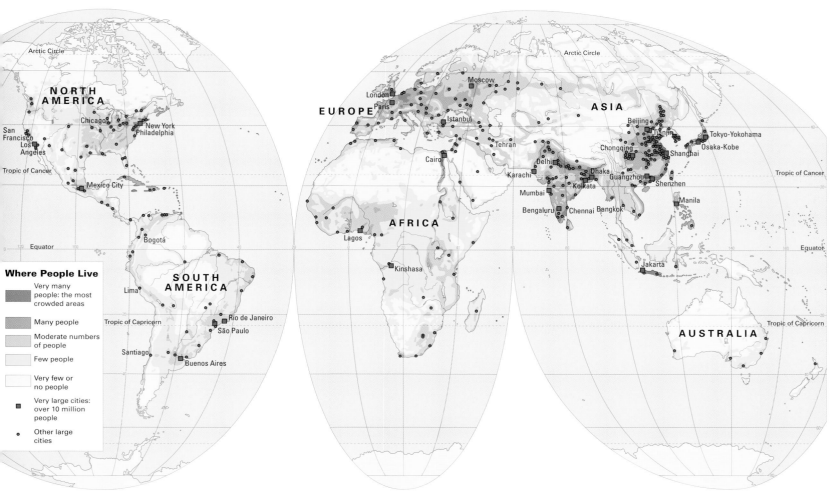

Where People Live

- Very many people: the most crowded areas
- Many people
- Moderate numbers of people
- Few people
- Very few or no people
- ■ Very large cities: over 10 million people
- • Other large cities

▲ **Empty and poor:** *a Tuareg nomad living in the Sahara desert, in Mali. It is hot and dusty and life is hard. The nomads move around with their animals.*

▲ **Crowded and rich:** *the skyscrapers of San Francisco seen from the bay. San Francisco is a city in California, on the west coast of the USA. Only the richest people can afford the apartments with the best views. The USA is the world's richest country, but there are poor people living in some areas of the cities.*

COLD AND HOT LANDS

FIVE important lines are drawn across these maps of the world: the Arctic and Antarctic Circles; the Tropics of Cancer and Capricorn; and the Equator. They divide the world roughly into *polar, temperate* and *tropical* zones.

The *polar* lands remain cold all through the year, even though the summer days are long and some snow melts.

The *temperate* lands have four seasons: summer and winter, with spring and autumn in between. But these seasons come at different times of the year north and south of the Equator. June is midwinter in southern lands.

The *tropical* lands are always hot, except where mountains or plateaus reach high above sea level. For some of the year the sun is directly overhead at noon (local time). Look at the **red** area on the maps.

The map on **this** page shows the world in June. Hardly anywhere is very cold (except for Antarctica in midwinter, of course). Most of the very hot areas in June are **north** of the Equator.

The December map (opposite page) is very different. Both Canada and Russia are **very** cold. Most of the hottest areas in December are **south** of the Equator, near the Tropic of Capricorn, because December is midsummer.

▲ **Arctic winter.** *Winter begins early in Greenland. This fishing boat is frozen in the harbour at Angmagssalik, near the Arctic Circle. There are 24 hours of dark and cold at Christmas. Yet by June, the ice will have melted, and there will be 24 hours of daylight.*

DID YOU KNOW?

Children in New Zealand open their Christmas presents on 25th December which is in midsummer!

Greenland

North of the Arctic Circle the Sun does not set at all on 21 June

Arctic Circle

EUROPE

Death Valley
The hottest place on Earth

NORTH

AMERICA

At the Tropic of Cancer the Sun shines right overhead at noon on 21 June

ASIA

Tropic of Cancer

Equator

AFRICA

Hot and Cold in June

SOUTH

AMERICA

Tropic of Capricorn

Very hot
Hot
Warm
Cool
Cold
Very cold
Frozen seas

Northern limit of snowfall

AUSTRALIA

Vostok
The coldest place on Earth

South of the Antarctic Circle the Sun does not even appear above the horizon on 21 June

Antarctic Circle

COPYRIGHT PHILIP'S

COLD & HOT LANDS FACTS

HOTTEST RECORDED TEMPERATURE
57°C at Death Valley in USA

COLDEST RECORDED TEMPERATURE
−89.2°C at Vostok in Antarctica

GREATEST CHANGE OF TEMPERATURE AT ONE PLACE IN A YEAR
From −70°C to +36.7°C at
Verkhoyansk in Siberia, Russia

▲ **In the hot, wet tropics,** trees grow tall and ferns grow fast. It is all green – and quite dark – in this forest on the island of Tobago, in the West Indies (see page 81).

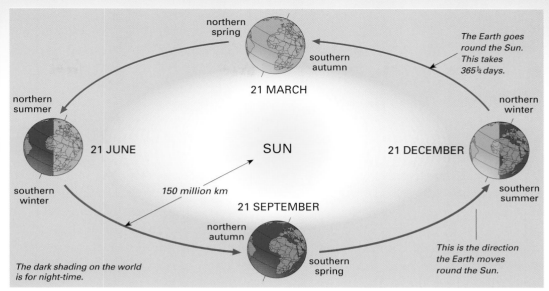

northern spring
southern autumn
21 MARCH

The Earth goes round the Sun. This takes 365¼ days.

northern summer
21 JUNE
southern winter

SUN

150 million km

northern winter
21 DECEMBER
southern summer

This is the direction the Earth moves round the Sun.

21 SEPTEMBER

northern autumn
southern spring

The dark shading on the world is for night-time.

The seasons are different north and south of the Equator. In June it is summer in North America, Europe and Asia. The sun is overhead at the Tropic of Cancer. The North Pole is tilted towards the sun, and the Arctic enjoys 24 hours of daylight. Notice that Antarctica is in total darkness.

By December, the Earth has travelled halfway round the sun. The sun is overhead at the Tropic of Capricorn. The South Pole is tilted towards the sun. Antarctica now has 24 hours of daylight, and it is summer in South America, southern Africa and Australia. But the Arctic is in total darkness and the Arctic Ocean is frozen.

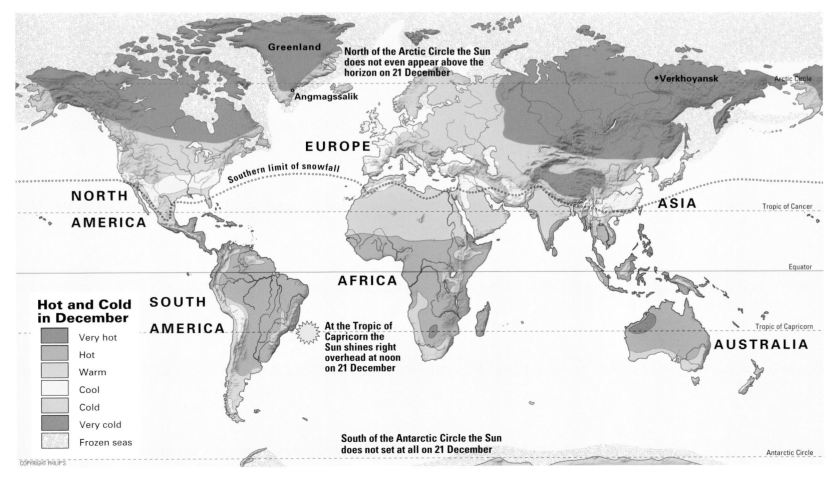

Greenland

North of the Arctic Circle the Sun does not even appear above the horizon on 21 December

•Verkhoyansk   Arctic Circle

°Angmagssalik

EUROPE

Southern limit of snowfall

NORTH
AMERICA   ASIA   Tropic of Cancer

                                                                    Equator

AFRICA

Hot and Cold in December

SOUTH
AMERICA

At the Tropic of Capricorn the Sun shines right overhead at noon on 21 December

Tropic of Capricorn

AUSTRALIA

- Very hot
- Hot
- Warm
- Cool
- Cold
- Very cold
- Frozen seas

South of the Antarctic Circle the Sun does not set at all on 21 December

Antarctic Circle

COPYRIGHT PHILIP'S

WET AND DRY LANDS

WATER is needed by all living things. But different parts of the world receive different amounts of water.

Follow the Equator on these two maps: the dark blue colour (below) shows heavy rain. Thick tropical forest grows here (page 15).

Now find the Tropics of Cancer and Capricorn: many parts are dry all year, and there are big deserts. Between the tropical forests and the deserts, there are 'savanna' areas, with tall grass and bushes: these areas have a wet and a dry season.

North of the Sahara Desert, near the Mediterranean Sea, it rains in winter. Summers are hot and dry.

In temperate lands, places near the oceans receive rain from the damp winds that blow from the sea all year. Trees grow well here. Far inland, it is much drier and there are vast grasslands, like the prairies of North America and the Russian steppes. In the centre of Asia, there is a desert with very cold winters.

Further north, temperate forests of pines and firs stretch right across North America, Europe and Asia.

In the far north, there is 'tundra', with no trees. The land is snow-covered for many months in winter, and marshy in the short summer.

Finally, Greenland and Antarctica are mostly snow and ice: find them on pages 88 and 89.

▲ *Forest and mountains in Alberta, Canada.* The coniferous trees can survive Canada's bitterly cold winters. In the high mountains, trees cannot grow: it is too cold and the soil is too thin. Can you see the forest across the lake?

Greenland

Arctic Circle

South-westerly Winds

EUROPE

South-westerly Winds

NORTH AMERICA

Gobi Desert

North-east Trade Winds

ASIA

Tropic of Cancer

Mount Wai-'ale-'ale

North-east Trade Winds

Arabian Desert

Sahara Desert

Cherrapunji
Yearly rainfall is often more than 1000 cm (400 inches) here

Tutunendo

AFRICA

South-east Trade Winds

Equator

South-east Trade Winds

South-east Trade Winds

Atacama Desert

SOUTH AMERICA

Kalahari Desert

Tropic of Capricorn

AUSTRALIA

Wet and Dry

- Very heavy rain
- Heavy rain
- Moderate rain
- Little rain
- Very little or no rain

Westerly Winds ('Roaring Forties')   Westerly Winds ('Roaring Forties')

Antarctic Circle

COPYRIGHT PHILIP'S

WET & DRY LANDS FACTS

HIGHEST RAINFALL IN ONE MONTH
9299 mm in one month at Cherrapunji, India

HIGHEST RAINFALL IN ONE YEAR
26,461 mm in one year at Cherrapunji

MOST RAINY DAYS
350 days in a year at Mount Wai-'ale-'ale in Hawaii

WETTEST PLACE ON AVERAGE
Over 11 metres of rain a year at Tutunendo, Colombia

DRIEST PLACE In the Atacama Desert, northern Chile: no rain for 400 years!

This map shows NATURAL vegetation – but in many places people have cut down forests to make farmland and towns. Most scientists now believe that pollution is changing the climates of the world: we can expect more storms, more floods, more droughts and hotter temperatures. As sea level rises, the lowest land near the sea is at risk from floods.

▲ **Burning the savanna, in northern Ghana, West Africa.** *At the end of the long dry season, farmers burn the bush (long grass and small trees). The land will be ready for planting crops when it rains. Sometimes, lightning can cause fires.*

▲ **Sand dunes in the desert in Namibia, southern Africa.** *The Namib Desert has given its name to the country of Namibia. It is a very dry area, west of the Kalahari Desert. But most of the world's desert areas are rocky, not sandy.*

Natural Vegetation
- Polar desert
- Tundra and mountain vegetation
- Temperate forest
- Temperate grassland
- Mediterranean vegetation
- Semi-desert, scrubland
- Hot desert
- Tropical grassland – savanna
- Tropical forest (jungle) and woodland

ENJOYING MAPS

COINS OF THE WORLD

The Ghana coin (left) shows cocoa pods growing on the branches of a cocoa tree. Cocoa is a major export from Ghana. Another Ghana coin (right) shows traditional drums.

Other countries also picture familiar items on their coins. **Nigeria** has a palm tree on its coins; **The Gambia** has a sailing ship on one of its coins (see page 53).

But don't believe everything you find on coins: some UK coins have pictures of lions, yet there are no wild lions there.

AN atlas is a book of maps. The maps in this book have been carefully drawn by cartographers (map-makers) to tell us about the countries of the world.

The maps on pages 6 to 15 show the whole world. Because the world is round, the best model is a globe. It is impossible to draw a really accurate map of the round world on a flat piece of paper. That is why the Pacific Ocean is cut in half, and Antarctica becomes a long thin strip. On pages 88 and 89 there are maps of parts of the world viewed from a different angle.

The maps on pages 18 to 89 show the continents and countries of the world. Each map has a key, with information that will help you 'read' the map. Use your imagination to 'see' what the land is like in each part of the world that you visit through these pages. The photos and text will make your picture clearer.

These two pages explain the key to all the maps. The country of GHANA is used as an example. Ghana is in square B2 of the map (right). Find Ⓑ at the top of the map with one finger, and ②➤ at the side of the map with another finger. Move each finger in the direction of the arrows; Ghana is where they meet.

The capital city of each country is underlined on the maps. The rulers of the country live in the capital city, and it is the biggest city in most countries. But not all capital cities are big. On this map, you can see three sizes of city. The biggest ones are marked by a square; they have the most people. Middle-sized cities have a big circle, and smaller cities have a small circle. Small towns and villages are not shown on maps of this scale, but some have been included in this atlas because they are mentioned in the text.

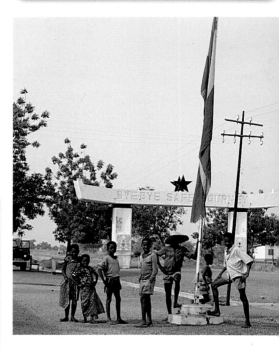

▲ **The border between Ghana and Burkina Faso.** *The red lines on the map show the borders between countries. When travelling from one country to another, you have to stop at the border. These children live in Ghana and their flag flies on their side of the border.*

'BYE-BYE SAFE JOURNEY' is the message on the arch. In Ghana, most officials speak English. In Burkina Faso officials speak French.

POSTAGE STAMPS ... are on some pages of this atlas

You can learn so much from stamps! The map shows you that Ghana is a country; the stamps tell you the official language of Ghana, and show you Ghana's flag.

The map tells you that Ghana has a coastline; the 10Np stamp tells you the name of Ghana's main port, and shows you the big modern cranes there.

The map shows that this port is very near to Accra, which is the capital city of Ghana.

The map tells you the name of Ghana's biggest lake (man-made). The 6Np stamp shows you the dam and its name.

You can see that they chose the narrowest part of the valley to build the dam. On page 57, there is a picture of a ferry on the lake.

Scale 1:20 000 000
0   200 km   400 km   600 km   800 km   1000 km   1200 km
1 cm on the map = 200 km on the ground
0   200 miles   400 miles   600 miles   800 miles
1 inch on the map = 320 miles on the ground

West from Greenwich 0° East from Greenwich

COPYRIGHT PHILIP'S

HEIGHT OF THE LAND

The countries of West Africa
are coloured so that you
can tell the height of the land.
Green shows the lowest land.
Often the real land will not look
green – in the dry season the
grass is brown. The higher land
is coloured brown, even though
some parts are covered with thick
green forest!

Height of the land
▲ Highest point on the map
over 6000 metres
4000 – 6000
2000 – 4000
1000 – 2000
400 – 1000
200 – 400
0 – 200 metres
sea level
below sea level

Country boundaries
Large cities
Capital cities underlined
Accra

   The highest point in West Africa is shown with a small
black triangle – find it in square C2. And to find land
below sea level (dark green) try page 25. In West Africa,
Cameroon has some dramatic mountains, but elsewhere
the change from lowland to highland is often quite gentle.
The 'shadows' on the map help you to see which mountains
have steep slopes.

   Blue means water: the oceans, big rivers and lakes.
Their names are in *italic print*, such as *Lake Volta* (B2).
Blue dashes show rivers which dry up in some years (B1).

   Find Lake Chad in square D1. Its size depends on how
much rain falls in the wet season.

SCALE

This box
shows the
scale of the
map. The scale
can be written
in different ways.

Scale 1:20 000 000
0   200 km   400 km   600 km   800 km   1000 km   1200 km
1 cm on the map = 200 km on the ground
0   200 miles   400 miles   600 miles   800 miles
1 inch on the map = 320 miles on the ground

   The map is drawn to a scale of 1:20,000,000, which
means that the distance between two places on the
ground is exactly 20 million times bigger than it is on
this page! Other maps in this atlas are drawn to different
scales: little Belgium (page 25) is drawn at a scale of
1:2 million, while the largest country in the world
is drawn at a scale of 1:45 million (Russia, page 41).
Another way of writing the scale of this map is to say
that 1 centimetre on the map is equal to 200 kilometres
on the ground in West Africa.

   You can use the scale line to make your own scale ruler.
Put the straight edge of a strip of paper against the scale
line and mark the position of 0, 200, 400, 600 kilometres,
etc. Carefully number each mark. Now move your scale
ruler over the map to see how far it is between places.
For example, Accra to Abidjan is 400 kilometres.

EUROPE

T HE map shows the great North European Plain that stretches from the Atlantic Ocean to the Ural Mountains in Russia. This huge area of lowland has most of Europe's best farmland, and many of the biggest cities.

To the north of the plain are the snowy mountains of Scandinavia. To the south are even higher mountains: the Pyrenees, the Alps and Carpathians, and the Caucasus Mountains. Southern Europe has hills and mountains by the Mediterranean Sea. The areas of lowland are carefully farmed.

PUZZLE

The most important building in Europe?
• Where is it found?
(*Answer on page 97.*)

EUROPE FACTS

AREA 10,531,000 sq km (including European Russia)
HIGHEST POINT Mt Elbrus (Russia), 5642 metres
LOWEST POINT By Caspian Sea, minus 38 metres
LONGEST RIVER Volga (Russia), 3690 km
LARGEST LAKE Caspian Sea*, 371,000 sq km
BIGGEST COUNTRY Russia*, 17,075,400 sq km (total area – Europe and Asia)
BIGGEST ALL-EUROPEAN COUNTRY Ukraine, 603,700 sq km
SMALLEST COUNTRY Vatican City* (in Rome, Italy), less than half a square kilometre!
MOST CROWDED COUNTRY Malta
LEAST CROWDED COUNTRY Iceland
* A world record as well as a European record

▲ **Northern Europe: Iceland.** *Lake Jokulsarlon has many small icebergs which break off the glacier that comes from the ice-cap. Ice melts to make the lake.*

▲ **Central Europe: Austria.** *These high mountains are called the Alps. In winter, there will be snow here. In summer, the grass is for the cows – can you see any?*

▲ **Southern Europe: Sardinia.** *The island of Sardinia is part of Italy and is in the Mediterranean. These children are enjoying their holiday in the hot sun.*

KEY
A. = ANDORRA
BOSNIA =
    BOSNIA–HERZEGOVINA
LI. = LIECHTENSTEIN
LUX. = LUXEMBOURG
M. = MONACO
MAC. = MACEDONIA
NETHS = NETHERLANDS
S.M. = SAN MARINO
V.C. = VATICAN CITY
* = Part of Azerbaijan
† = Part of Russia

Scale 1:30 000 000

0   300 km   600 km   900 km   1200 km   1500 km

1 cm on the map = 300 km on the ground

0   300 miles   600 miles   900 miles

1 inch on the map = 480 miles on the ground

Europe in the World

COPYRIGHT PHILIP'S

The countries of Georgia, Armenia and Azerbaijan are really in Asia but are also included on this map because it is at a larger scale.

SCANDINAVIA

FINLAND

AREA 338,145 sq km
POPULATION 5,537,000
MONEY Euro

DENMARK

AREA 43,094 sq km
POPULATION 5,810,000
MONEY Danish krone

THE five countries that make up Scandinavia are rich and successful, yet the people live further north than in almost any other part of the world.

The total population of each of these countries is small, and very few people live in the far north. Most people live in towns and cities, with excellent central heating in their houses and flats.

Farming is difficult this far north because the winters are long and cold. Scandinavia has hardly any minerals except for iron ore in **Sweden** and oil under the North Sea.

The mountains of **Iceland** and **Norway** are high and rugged, making travel difficult. There are large ice-sheets and glaciers in the highest areas of both countries. Iceland has many volcanoes.

▲ *Geiranger fjord, Norway, is one of many long, narrow inlets of the sea along the Norwegian coast. Glaciers dug these deep, steep valleys. The village is on the flat land at the head of the fjord. The steep mountains mean that the best way to travel is often by boat.*

LEGOLAND MODEL VILLAGE

Lego was invented by a toymaker in Denmark. Legoland Denmark has a model Village near the factory. There are models of famous buildings as well as ordinary houses from different parts of the world. The photograph shows the model of a typical fishing village in the Lofoten Islands, which are off the northern coast of Norway. The Lego man and his friends can be found in shops all over the world!

▲ *Reindeer in Lapland. Lapland is the northern part of Norway, Sweden and Finland, where the Lapps (Saami) live. They keep reindeer for their milk, meat and leather, and to pull sledges. They search under the snow for lichen and other food. In winter, it is dark here even at midday, but in summer it is light at midnight.*

▲ *Lake Saimaa, Finland, is one of hundreds of lakes in the southern part of that country. Only the largest are shown on the map. During the Ice Age, ice-sheets scraped hollows in the rock which filled with water after the ice melted. Many families own a summer cottage among the trees beside a lake.*

NORWAY

AREA 323,877 sq km
POPULATION 5,372,000
MONEY Norwegian krone

SWEDEN

AREA 449,964 sq km
POPULATION 10,041,000
MONEY Swedish krona

Denmark, Finland and southern Sweden are low-lying. The soil is formed from sand, gravel and clay brought by ice-sheets in the Ice Age. There are large lakes in Sweden. Some people have holiday homes on their shores.

The islands of Denmark are now linked by big bridges. Since 2000, Denmark and Sweden have been connected by road and rail through a tunnel 4 km long and over a bridge nearly 8 km long.

▲ **Stockholm harbour, Sweden:** *this fine nineteenth-century sailing ship is now a Youth Hostel for visitors to the capital city of Sweden. Stockholm is a seaport with a large harbour. It is built on lots of islands and the nearby mainland, so there are many bridges.*

LAND OF ICE AND FIRE

The volcanoes of Iceland are mostly quiet and peaceful (above left). But sometimes a great volcanic eruption lights up the night sky and the light is reflected in the sea (above right). Ash can shoot high in the sky.

Only 332,000 people live in Iceland. It is near the Arctic Circle and there is ice on the mountains, in glaciers and ice-sheets. A warm Atlantic current keeps the sea ice-free and it is full of fish. Iceland has an important fishing fleet.

Scale 1:10 000 000

0   100 km   200 km   300 km   400 km

1 cm on the map = 100 km on the ground

0   100 miles   200 miles

1 inch on the map = 160 miles on the ground

Height of the land

over 6000 metres	
4000 – 6000	
2000 – 4000	
1000 – 2000	
400 – 1000	
200 – 400	
0 – 200 metres	
below sea level	

▲ Highest point on the map

sea level

Icefield

Country boundaries

■ ▣ ● Large cities

Oslo Capital cities underlined

COPYRIGHT PHILIP'S

THE UK AND IRELAND

UK

AREA 241,857 sq km
POPULATION 65,105,000
MONEY Pound sterling
CAPITAL London

THE United Kingdom (UK) is made up of Great Britain (England, Wales and Scotland) and Northern Ireland. The UK parliament meets in London, but Wales, Scotland and Northern Ireland have their own parliaments.

Look at the high land on the map: it is in the north and west of Great Britain, where the rocks are older and harder than in the south and east. Many old factories and mines were in the north and west on the coalfields and they have closed now. The higher land gets more rain, and has pasture for cattle and sheep. Most of the arable farming is in the lower, drier and flatter south and east of Britain.

▲ **Windsor Castle** is the oldest and largest castle in the world that is still lived in. It is the official home of the Queen, although she also has palaces in London and Edinburgh. Windsor is a small town beside the River Thames, west of London. Tourists come from all over the world to visit historic places, and the 'tourist industry' is very important for the UK.

▲ **The city of Newcastle** has many bridges over the River Tyne. This steel arch is the same design as the Sydney Harbour bridge in Australia.

IRELAND

AREA 70,273 sq km
POPULATION 5,068,000
MONEY Euro
CAPITAL Dublin

▲ **A reservoir in Wales** where the River Elan is held back by the Craig Goch dam (Welsh for 'Red Rock'). The water is piped from Wales, in the wetter west, to Birmingham. It is also used to make electricity.

LONDON

Can you spot 8 famous historic London landmarks? (Answer on page 97.)

▲ **Dublin, the capital of Ireland.** This air-photo shows us that Dublin is built on both sides of the River Liffey. How many bridges can you see? A quarter of Ireland's population lives in Dublin and its suburbs.

▲ **The Somerset Levels,** south of Bristol in south-west England. The foreground was marshland which has been drained — it is below the level of high tides.

CAN YOU FIND THESE ON THE MAP?

Highest mountain – Ben Nevis
Longest river – Shannon
Largest lake – Lough Neagh
Greenwich Meridian – 0°

Ireland is a completely separate country from the UK although it was part of Britain until 1922. Its money is the Euro. It also has its own language, Irish, though everyone speaks English too. There were twice as many people in Ireland 180 years ago as there are today. Many Irish people emigrated to the UK or USA to find work. Farming is still important, but new factories have been built in many towns.

▲ **The Highlands of Scotland** are very beautiful. The hard rocks are hundreds of millions of years old, and they were eroded by glaciers in the Ice Age.

Scale 1:5 000 000

1 cm on the map = 50 km on the ground
1 inch on the map = 80 miles on the ground

Height of the land

▲ Highest point on the map

over 6000 metres
4000 – 6000
2000 – 4000
1000 – 2000
400 – 1000
200 – 400
0 – 200 metres
below sea level

Country boundaries
Large cities
London Capital cities underlined

COPYRIGHT PHILIP'S

BENELUX

BELGIUM

AREA 30,528 sq km
POPULATION 11,571,000
MONEY Euro

NETHERLANDS

AREA 41,526 sq km
POPULATION 17,151,000
MONEY Euro

BENELUX is a word made up from BElgium, NEtherlands and LUXembourg. Fortunately, the first two letters of each name are the same in most languages, so everyone can understand the word. These three countries agreed to co-operate soon after World War 2. But they still have their very own Kings (of Belgium and of the Netherlands), and Grand Duke (of Luxembourg). Look at the coins below.

The Benelux countries are all small and are the most crowded in mainland Europe, but there is plenty of countryside too. Most of the land is low and flat, so they are sometimes called the Low Countries.

▲ *Are these windmills?* Most Dutch 'windmills' are really wind-pumps. They were used to pump water up from the fields into rivers and canals. The river is higher than the land! These are at Kinderdijk, east of Rotterdam.

GAINING LAND

The map shows that a large part of the Netherlands is below sea level. For over 1000 years, the Dutch have built dykes (embankments) to keep out the sea and rivers. Then the water is pumped out to create dry land called 'polders'. Once they used wind-pumps (see photo above); today they use diesel or electric pumps. The rich farmland grows vegetables and flowers.

LUXEMBOURG

AREA 2,586 sq km
POPULATION 606,000
MONEY Euro

▲ *Bruges* is a historic town in Belgium. This horse-drawn carriage is taking tourists round the medieval market square. Look at the 'stepped' gables of the old buildings behind the market stalls.

WHICH COUNTRY?

These Euro coins come from the Benelux countries – but which coin belongs to which country? The Dutch coin shows Queen Beatrix who reigned until 2013. (*Answers on page 97.*)

▲ *Europort, Rotterdam.* Rotterdam is by far the biggest port in Europe. Ships come from all over the world, and barges travel along the River Rhine and the canals of Europe to reach the port. Containers unloaded from this ship may be taken to other ports around the North Sea.

PUZZLE

A puzzle from the Netherlands: What are these round yellow items for sale in a market? (Some have been cut and sliced.)

(*Answer on page 97.*)

Belgium is *one* country with *two* languages. South of Brussels most people speak French. In the north they speak Flemish (similar to Dutch). Road signs in Belgium are in both languages.

Brussels is an important city. It is the capital of Belgium and the headquarters of the whole European Union.

The eastern part of the **Netherlands** has large areas of heath and forest.

But the best-known Dutch landscape is the 'polders' of the west. Look at the map to see how much of the land is *below* sea level – and threatened with floods if the sea level rises. But this is the country's best farmland.

Scale 1:2 000 000

0   20 km   40 km   60 km   80 km   100 km

1 cm on the map = 20 km on the ground

0   20 miles   40 miles   60 miles

1 inch on the map = 32 miles on the ground

Height of the land

over 6000 metres
4000 – 6000
2000 – 4000
1000 – 2000
400 – 1000
200 – 400
0 – 200 metres
below sea level

▲ Highest point on the map

sea level

Country boundaries
Large cities
Brussels Capital cities underlined

Frisian Islands
Wadden Zee

Groningen
Leeuwarden

Den Helder

GERMANY

IJssel L.

Alkmaar

Edam
Zwolle

Polders

Haarlem   **Amsterdam**

Enschede

N E T H E R L A N D S

The Hague   Leiden   Amersfoort   Apeldoorn
Utrecht

North Sea

Hook of Holland   Gouda   *Lek*   Arnhem
Europoort

Rotterdam   *Waal*
Dordrecht   Nijmegen

Rhine

Breda   Tilburg

Maas

Walcheren

Eindhoven

Zeebrugge

Ostend   Bruges   **Antwerp**

F l a n d e r s   Ghent

Brussels

Maastricht

B E L G I U M

Liège

Meuse

Mons   Namur   ▲ 694

Charleroi

F R A N C E

A r d e n n e s

LUXEMBOURG

Luxembourg

COPYRIGHT PHILIP'S

▲ *Vianden Castle, Luxembourg,* *is one of many castles overlooking the wooded valleys of the Ardennes. This one was built in the eleventh century and has recently been restored.*

Amsterdam is the capital city of the Netherlands, but the parliament meets in The Hague.

FRANCE

FRANCE

AREA 551,500 sq km
POPULATION 67,364,000
MONEY Euro

The French flag is called the 'tricolore'. It has been used since the French Revolution in 1789.

FRANCE is a country with three coastlines: can you see which these are? It is hot in summer in the south, but usually cool in the mountains and in the north. France is the biggest country in Western Europe, so there are big contrasts between north and south.

The highest mountains are the Alps in the south-east and the Pyrenees in the south-west. They are popular for skiing in winter and for summer holidays too.

More than half the country is lowland, with wide rivers. Farming is very important: besides fruit and vegetables, France is famous for its many different cheeses and wines, as well as delicious *cuisine* (cooking).

▲ **Mont Blanc.** *The 'White Mountain' is the highest mountain in Western Europe. It is 4808 metres high. Even in summer (as here) it is covered in snow. Cable-cars take tourists and skiers up the mountain. There is a road tunnel through Mont Blanc to Italy.*

▲ **The Eiffel Tower** *was built in Paris in 1889. It was designed by Monsieur Eiffel, an engineer. It is 300 metres high and weighs 7000 tonnes! Lifts go to the top.*

▲ **Market at Grasse.** *Some of this lovely fruit has been grown in the warm sunshine of the south of France. Every town in France has a good market selling fresh produce.*

▲ **The Camargue** *is a wetland area in the delta of the River Rhône. It is important for wildlife.*

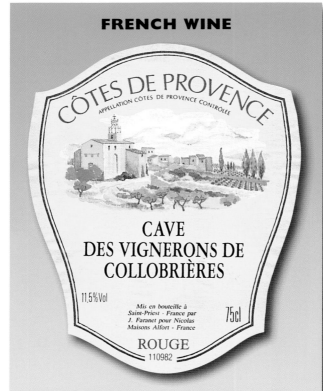

FRENCH WINE

CÔTES DE PROVENCE
APPELLATION CÔTES DE PROVENCE CONTRÔLÉE

CAVE
DES VIGNERONS DE
COLLOBRIÈRES

11,5%Vol

Mis en bouteille à Saint-Priest - France par J. Faranet pour Nicolas Maisons Alfort - France

75cl

ROUGE
110982

This label is from a bottle of red wine from Provence, in the south of France. It tells you where the grapes were grown and where the wine was bottled. Collobrières is a village east of the River Rhône. The houses have red tiled roofs. Around the village are fields of fruit trees and vines. Rows of tall trees have been planted to shelter the crops from cold winds. The red grapes are picked in the autumn.

The biggest city is Paris, which is also the capital and the official home of the French President. Ten million people live in the Paris region. Five big new towns have been built, linked to the city centre by fast trains.

Tourists come to Paris from all over the world. Here, you can enjoy a boat trip on the River Seine past Notre Dame Cathedral on the Ile de France, or travel east to the Disneyland Resort, Paris.

CAN YOU FIND...

the names of long rivers that flow from the...

- Alps to the Mediterranean
- Pyrenees to the Bay of Biscay
- hills of Burgundy to the Channel

FRANCE

Height of the land

	over 6000 metres
	3000 – 6000
	2000 – 3000
	1000 – 2000
	400 – 1000
	200 – 400
	0 – 200 metres
	below sea level

▲ Highest point on the map

sea level

Country boundaries
Large cities
Paris Capital city underlined

Scale 1:5 000 000

| 0 | 50 km | 100 km | 150 km | 200 km | 250 km |

1 cm on the map = 50 km on the ground

| 0 | 50 miles | 100 miles | 150 miles |

1 inch on the map = 80 miles on the ground

See page 33 for Corsica

COPYRIGHT PHILIP'S

27

GERMANY AND AUSTRIA

GERMANY

AREA 357,022 sq km
POPULATION 80,458,000
MONEY Euro

AUSTRIA

AREA 83,859 sq km
POPULATION 8,793,000
MONEY Euro

▲ *Berlin:* this ruined tower, next to the new tower of the Memorial Church, is left as a reminder of the destruction caused by war. It is in the city centre. Berlin is no longer divided and is once again the capital of a united Germany.

GERMANY has more people than any other European country apart from Russia. Most of the 81 million Germans live in towns and cities. Several million people called 'guest workers' have come from southern Europe and Turkey to work in Germany's factories. But nowadays there is unemployment in Germany, as in other European countries, and many 'guest workers' have returned home. Among the many different goods made in Germany there are excellent cars: Audi, BMW, Mercedes, Opel, Porsche and Volkswagen.

There is also plenty of beautiful and uncrowded countryside. The north is mostly lowland. Parts of the south, such as the Black Forest, are mountainous and popular for holidays.

Germany was one country from 1870 to 1945. In 1990 it became one country again. From 1945 until 1990, it was divided into West Germany and East Germany, and there was a border fence between the two. In Berlin, the high wall that divided the city into east and west was knocked down in 1989. It became the capital city again in 2000.

▲ *Edelweiss* are flowers that grow high in the Alps. They can survive in thin soil on steep slopes, and do not mind being buried by snow all winter. They are a national symbol in Austria.

▲ *The Rhine Gorge*, in western Germany. Castles once guarded this important river route. The River Rhine flows from Switzerland, through Germany to the Netherlands. Big barges travel between the ports and factories beside the river. Tourists travel along the river to enjoy the beautiful landscape.

TRANSPORT

Germany has excellent roads and railways. The picture above shows two inter-city express (ICE) trains passing on a bridge over an *autobahn* (motorway).

This cable-car (left) is in Austria. Tourists can ride high into the Alps to ski in winter and walk in summer. The Alps continue into Switzerland and Italy (p.33) and France (p.27).

AUSTRIA: Until 1918, Austria and Hungary were linked, and together ruled a great empire which included much of Central Europe and Slovenia, Croatia and Bosnia (see page 34). But now Austria is a small, peaceful country.

Most Austrians live in the lower eastern part of the country. The capital is Vienna, on the River Danube. Many famous composers have lived in this city. It was once at the centre of the Austrian Empire: now it is in a corner of the country.

In the west of Austria are the high Alps. Many tourists come to enjoy the beautiful scenery and winter sports. Busy motorways and electric railways cross the Austrian Alps to link Germany with Italy.

WHO ARE THE NEIGHBOURS?

Nine countries have borders with Germany – Austria is one of them. Try to name the others – then check your answer on the map on page 19.

▲ *Hallstatt, Austria,* is built on steep slopes which are part of the Dachstein Mountains in the eastern Alps, south-east of Salzburg. It lies beside a deep blue lake with the same name. There is plenty of snow in winter.

Scale 1:5 000 000

| 0 | 50 km | 100 km | 150 km | 200 km | 250 km |

1 cm on the map = 50 km on the ground

| 0 | 50 miles | 100 miles | 150 miles |

1 inch on the map = 80 miles on the ground

Height of the land

▲ Highest point on the map	over 6000 metres
	3000 – 6000
	2000 – 3000
	1000 – 2000
	400 – 1000
	200 – 400
	0 – 200 metres
	below sea level

Country boundaries
Large cities
Capital cities underlined
Vienna

COPYRIGHT PHILIP'S

29

SPAIN AND PORTUGAL

SPAIN

AREA 497,548 sq km
POPULATION 48,958,000
MONEY Euro

PORTUGAL

AREA 88,797 sq km
POPULATION 10,355,000
MONEY Euro

S PAIN and Portugal are separated from the rest of Europe by the high Pyrenees Mountains. Most people travelling by land from the north reach Spain along the Atlantic or Mediterranean coasts.

The Meseta is the very high plateau of central Spain. Winters are very cold, and summers are very hot. The capital city, Madrid, is about 650 metres above sea level. Olives and grapes are the main crops, and both Spain and Portugal export famous wines such as sherry and port. Cars are a major export from Spain nowadays. Both Spain and Portugal have fine cities with great churches and cathedrals, built when they were the richest countries in the world.

▲ **Benidorm on the Costa Blanca** ('White Coast') is a famous tourist resort in Spain. Until the 1960s Benidorm was a quiet fishing village. Since then, all these skyscrapers have been built as hotels and apartments for tourists who come by aeroplane to enjoy the sun, sea and sand.

▲ **Portuguese fishermen** mending their nets at Tavira, on the Algarve. They continue to land sardines and other fish, but the town relies on the tourist trade for most of its income.

DID YOU KNOW?

Gibraltar is still a British colony, but it is only 6 square kilometres in area. Spain still owns two towns in Morocco: **Ceuta** and **Melilla**. Spain wants Gibraltar – and Morocco wants Ceuta and Melilla. The argument has been going on for nearly 300 years....

THE ALHAMBRA PALACE

This beautiful palace in Granada, Spain, was built by the Moors (Arabs from North Africa). The Moors ruled southern Spain for hundreds of years, until 1492. The Arabs brought new ideas and new crops to Europe, such as oranges, rice and sugar-cane, which are still grown in Spain today.

The photo (left) of the Court of Lions shows the stone lions carved 600 years ago by Arab craftsmen.

▲ **Village in southern Spain.** The old houses crowd closely together, and roads are very narrow: wide enough for a donkey, but not for lorries. People whitewash their houses to reflect the rays of the hot sun. Some of the roofs are used as balconies.

SPAIN AND PORTUGAL

People visit **Spain** for holidays: the Costa Brava (Rugged Coast), Costa Blanca (White Coast), Costa del Sol (Coast of the Sun) and the Balearic Islands (Majorca, Minorca and Ibiza).

People also enjoy holidays in the **Canary Islands**. These belong to Spain – find them on page 55. These volcanic islands have fertile soil. Some have lava cones and black sand.

In **Portugal** the Algarve coast is the most popular holiday area. **Madeira** is a Portuguese island far out in the Atlantic Ocean (see page 55). It is another holiday area that is also famous for its wine.

ATLANTIC OCEAN

Bay of Biscay

C. Finisterre

La Coruña
Santiago
Vigo
Orense
Minho
Cantabrian Mountains
Gijón
Oviedo
León
Burgos
Valladolid
Duero
Old Castile
Santander
Bilbao
San Sebastián
Basque Provinces
Vitoria
Pamplona
Navarre
Ebro
Pyrenees
Andorra La-Vella
ANDORRA
Aragon
Zaragoza
Lérida
Catalonia
F R A N C E
Costa Brava

Oporto
Douro
PORTUGAL
Salamanca
Sierra de Guadarrama
Madrid
Toledo
Tagus
S P A I N
Barcelona
Tarragona

Coimbra
Nazaré
Tagus
Santarém
Lisbon
Évora
Extramadura
Cáceres
Badajoz
New Castile
Guadiana
Meseta
Sierra Morena
Linares
Castellón
Valencia
Gulf of Valencia
Júcar
Albacete
C. de la Nao
Benidorm
Alicante
Elche
Segura
Murcia
Costa Blanca
Cartagena
Balearic Islands
Palma
Majorca
Ibiza

Algarve
Lagos
Faro
Tavira
Huelva
Seville
Andalusia
Córdoba
Guadalquivir
Granada
Sierra Nevada
Mulhacén 3478
Almería
Gulf of Cadiz
Jérez
Cádiz
Marbella
Málaga
Costa del Sol
Gibraltar (U.K.)
Ceuta (Sp.)
Alborán (Sp.)
Mediterranean Sea
Minorca
Majorca

Melilla (Sp.)

M O R O C C O
A L G E R I A

West from Greenwich 0° East from Greenwich

Scale 1:5 000 000

0   50 km   100 km   150 km   200 km   250 km

1 cm on the map = 50 km on the ground

0   50 miles   100 miles   150 miles

1 inch on the map = 80 miles on the ground

Height of the land

- over 6000 metres
- 3000 – 6000
- 2000 – 3000
- 1000 – 2000
- 400 – 1000
- 200 – 400
- 0 – 200 metres
- below sea level

▲ Highest point on the map

Country boundaries
● ● Large cities
Madrid Capital cities underlined

COPYRIGHT PHILIP'S

31

SWITZERLAND AND ITALY

SWITZERLAND

AREA 41,284 sq km
POPULATION 8,293,000
MONEY Swiss franc

▲ **The Matterhorn** in the Swiss Alps is 4478 metres high. Glaciers helped carve its shape. Zermatt is the ski resort which gives good views of the peak.

ITALY is shaped like a boot: its toe seems to be kicking Sicily! The shape is caused by the long range of fold mountains called the Apennines. The great Roman Empire was centred on Italy, and there are many Roman ruins. Yet Italy was only united as a country less than 150 years ago. Italy has lots of big factories. The Fiat car plant in Turin is one of the largest in the world.

The south of Italy and the islands of Sicily and Sardinia have hot, dry summers. These areas are much less rich than the north. Many people have moved to the industrial cities in the north of the country to find work. But government projects are bringing factories and better roads.

In **Switzerland**, most people live in cities north of the Alps. Switzerland is one of the world's richest countries, with modern banks, offices and factories. Rivers, dams and waterfalls in the Alps are used for making hydro-electric power: trains, factories and homes in Switzerland all run on cheap electricity. Cable-cars powered by electricity take skiers and tourists high into the beautiful mountains. Switzerland holds some amazing world records (see below).

▲ **Venice,** in north-east Italy, is a city built in the sea. Everywhere in the old town has to be reached by boat, or on foot, because the 'roads' are canals.

ITALIAN FOOD

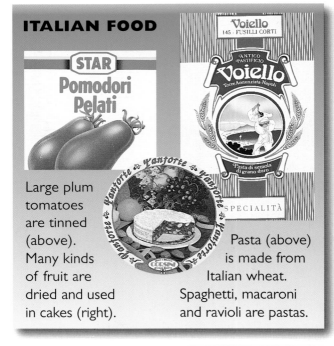

Large plum tomatoes are tinned (above). Many kinds of fruit are dried and used in cakes (right).

Pasta (above) is made from Italian wheat. Spaghetti, macaroni and ravioli are pastas.

WORLD RECORDS IN SWITZERLAND

- The longest and deepest rail tunnel in the world runs through the Alps: the Gotthard Base Tunnel opened in 2016 and is 57 kilometres long.
- The longest stairway is beside the Niesenbahn mountain railway, near Spiez. It has 11,674 steps!
- The steepest railway goes up Mount Pilatus. It has a gradient of 48%.
- Switzerland has been at peace with everyone since 1815. That's quite a record!

▲ **Vinci, Tuscany,** is a small town west of Florence. It was once the home of the famous artist Leonardo. The roofs are covered with pantiles. Lots of olive trees are growing in the fields below the town.

ITALY

AREA 301,318 sq km
POPULATION 62,247,000
MONEY Euro

OTHER COUNTRIES ON THIS MAP:
Vatican City in Rome;
San Marino within Italy;
Malta, an island country south of Italy.

A U S T R I A

SWITZERLAND

Basle
Winterthur
Zurich
St. Gallen
LIECHTENSTEIN
Berne
Pilatus
Luzern
Lausanne
Spiez
Interlaken
Geneva
L. Geneva
Rhône
Gotthard Tunnel
A l p s
A l p s
SWITZERLAND
Matterhorn 4478
Mte Rosa 4634
L. Maggiore
Lugano
L. Como
Bolzano
Trento
Udine
SLOVENIA

F R A N C E

Milan
Brescia
L. Garda
Vicenza
Trieste
Turin
Verona
Padua
Venice
Po
Po
Parma
Modena
Bologna
Ravenna
Genoa
La Spezia
Rimini
Gulf of Genoa
SAN MARINO
MONACO
Pisa
Florence
Ancona
Livorno
Siena
Perugia
Sorano
Bastia
Elba

Corsica
(France)
Ajaccio

Str. of Bonifacio

L i g u r i a n   S e a

A p e n n i n e s

Terni
Celano
Pescara

VATICAN CITY
Rome
Foggia

Bari
Olbia
Naples
Vesuvius
Brindisi
Sassari
Ischia
Salerno
Taranto
Capri

Sardinia
(Italy)

CROATIA

A l b a n i a

A d r i a t i c   S e a

Strait of Otranto

GREECE

Gulf of Taranto

Cosenza

Cagliari

T y r r h e n i a n   S e a

I o n i a n   S e a

M e d i t e r r a n e a n   S e a

Lipari Is.

Palermo
Messina
Reggio
Egadi Is.
Mt. Etna
Str. of Messina
S i c i l y
Catania
Siracusa
Pantelleria

TUNISIA

Gozo
MALTA   Valletta

Satellite image to match with the map.
The clouds are white, but what makes the brown smoke?
(Answer on page 97.)

Height of the land

▲ Highest point on the map

over 6000 metres
3000 – 6000
2000 – 3000
1000 – 2000
400 – 1000
200 – 400
0 – 200 metres
sea level
below sea level

Country boundaries
Large cities
Rome Capital cities underlined

Scale 1:5 500 000

| 0 | 50 km | 100 km | 150 km | 200 km | 250 km |

1 cm on the map = 55 km on the ground

| 0 | 50 miles | 100 miles | 150 miles |

1 inch on the map = 87 miles on the ground

East from Greenwich

COPYRIGHT PHILIP'S

SOUTH-EAST EUROPE

GREECE

AREA 131,957 sq km
POPULATION 10,762,000
MONEY Euro

BULGARIA

AREA 110,912 sq km
POPULATION 7,058,000
MONEY Lev

ALBANIA

AREA 28,748 sq km
POPULATION 3,057,000
MONEY Lek

MOST of south-east Europe is very mountainous, except near the River Danube. Farmers keep sheep and goats in the mountains and grow grain, vines and sunflowers on the lower land.

The coastlines are popular with tourists. There are many holiday resorts beside the Adriatic Sea (**Croatia**), the Aegean Sea (**Greece** and **Turkey**), and the Black Sea (**Romania** and **Bulgaria**). The Romanians are building new ski villages in their mountains. All these countries are trying to develop new industries, but this is still one of the poorest parts of Europe.

Albania is one of the least-known countries in Europe, although it is now slowly opening up to visits from tourists.

Yugoslavia no longer exists. It was 1 country with 2 alphabets (Latin and Cyrillic), 3 religious groups (Roman Catholic, Orthodox and Muslim), and 4 languages. Now there are 7 countries: **Slovenia**, **Croatia**, **Serbia**, **Montenegro**, **Kosovo**, **Bosnia-Herzegovina** and **Macedonia**.

▲ *The town of Korcula, in Croatia,* is built on an island – also called Korcula – in the Adriatic Sea, north-west of Dubrovnik. In the distance are the limestone mountains of the mainland. Until 1991, Croatia was part of Yugoslavia, but after some fighting it became independent.

THE CORINTH CANAL

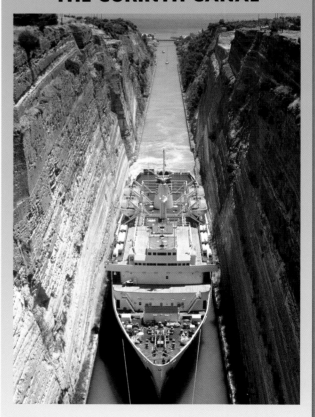

A cruise ship being towed through the Corinth Canal in southern Greece. The canal was cut in 1893 and is 6.4 kilometres long. It links the Gulf of Corinth with the Aegean Sea.

THE DANUBE

This stamp shows a boat at the gorge on the River Danube called the Iron Gates, on the southern border of Romania. The Danube flows from Germany to a marshy delta beside the Black Sea.

▲ *Harvest time in Romania.* The tomato harvest is being gathered by hand on a hot summer day. The horse-drawn cart will take the full boxes back to the village for distribution.

Α Β Γ Δ Ε Ζ Η Θ Ι Κ Λ Μ Ν Ξ Ο Π Ρ Σ Τ Υ Φ Χ Ψ Ω

A V/B G D E Z E TH I K L M N X O P R S T Y F CH PS O

▲ **The Greek alphabet:** *the Greeks developed their alphabet before the Romans, and they still use it. Some letters are the same as ours (A, B ...), and some look the same but have a different sound (P, H ...). The other letters are completely different. Some Greek letters appear in the Cyrillic alphabet, which is used in Bulgaria, the former Yugoslavia, and Russia (see page 41). The word 'alphabet' is formed from the first two Greek letters: alpha and beta. The Greek letter for D is called 'delta': also the name for some river mouths that have a similar shape (page 96).*

▲ **The Acropolis of Athens, Greece.** *The monuments on this hill above the capital city are the ruins of temples built about 2400 years ago. Ruins of ancient Greek cities can be found in many of the countries shown on the map.*

Scale 1:10 000 000

| 0 | 100 km | 200 km | 300 km | 400 km | 500 km |

1 cm on the map = 100 km on the ground

| 0 | 100 miles | 200 miles | 300 miles |

1 inch on the map = 160 miles on the ground

Height of the land

- over 6000 metres
- 4000 – 6000
- 2000 – 4000
- 1000 – 2000
- 400 – 1000
- 200 – 400
- 0 – 200 metres
- below sea level

▲ Highest point on the map

sea level

Country boundaries
Large cities
Athens Capital cities underlined

GERMANY
SLOVAKIA
AUSTRIA
HUNGARY
SLOVENIA
Ljubljana
CROATIA
Zagreb
Drava
Belgrade
BOSNIA-HERZEGOVINA
Dinaric Alps
Sarajevo
SERBIA
Split
Adriatic Sea
Korcula
Dubrovnik
MONTENEGRO
Podgorica
Nis
KOSOVO
Pristina
Skopje
MACEDONIA
Bitola
Tirane
ALBANIA
ITALY
Ionian Is.
Corfu
Pindus Mts
GREECE
Ionian Sea
Patrai
G. of Corinth
Corinth Canal
Athens
Mikonos
C. Tainaron
MALTA
ROMANIA
Cluj
Timisoara
Transylvanian Alps
Brasov
Iron Gates
Moreva
Craiova
Danube
Ruse
Balkan Mts.
Sofia
BULGARIA
Musala 2925
Plovdiv
Thessaloniki
Volos
Aegean Sea
Dardanelles
TURKEY
Carpathians
Prut
Iasi
MOLDOVA
UKRAINE
Galati
Ploiesti
Bucharest
Constanta
Black Sea
Varna
Burgas
Bosporus
TURKEY
Dodecanese
Rhodes
CYPRUS
Crete
Iraklion
Mediterranean Sea

EASTERN EUROPE

POLAND

AREA 323,250 sq km
POPULATION 38,421,000
MONEY Zloty

HUNGARY

AREA 93,032 sq km
POPULATION 9,826,000
MONEY Forint

UKRAINE

AREA 603,700 sq km
POPULATION 43,952,000
MONEY Hryvnia

SEVEN countries from Eastern Europe joined the European Union in 2004: Estonia, Latvia, Lithuania, Poland, Czechia, Slovakia and Hungary.

Poland has a coastline on the Baltic Sea. There are huge shipbuilding factories at Gdansk. Towns in the south have big factories, too, where there is plenty of coal. Most of Poland is flat farmland. The magnificent mountains in the far south are being 'rediscovered' by tourists.

Czechoslovakia split into two countries in 1993. Czechia is west of Slovakia. Both countries have beautiful hills and mountains, with fine pine trees. Skoda cars come from Czechia. Further south is Hungary, a small country with SEVEN neighbours – can you name them? Most of Hungary is good farmland on plains and hills.

Polish, Czech and Slovak are all Slavic languages. Hungarian is totally different: it came from central Asia. Some Hungarian speakers also live in Slovakia and Romania.

Six countries on this map were part of the USSR (Soviet Union) until 1991.

▲ **Town square in Telc, Czechia.**
These houses date from the 1500s, when the town was rebuilt after a great fire. This is a popular place for tourists to visit. The historic centres of many towns in Eastern Europe are carefully preserved. Some have been totally rebuilt in the old style after wartime bombing.

BELARUS

AREA 207,600 sq km
POPULATION 9,528,000
MONEY Belarusian ruble

CZECHIA

AREA 78,866 sq km
POPULATION 10,686,000
MONEY Czech koruna

SLOVAKIA

AREA 49,012 sq km
POPULATION 5,446,000
MONEY Euro

▲ **Church in Ukraine,** *where many people are Orthodox Christians. The Ukraine is Europe's biggest country, apart from Russia. The population is nearly as big as the UK or France.*

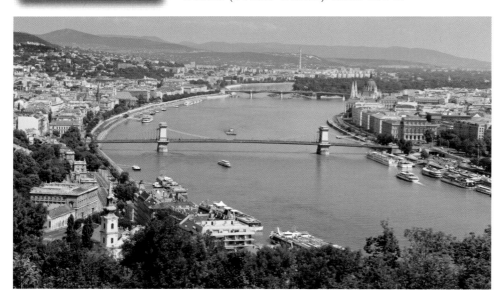

▲ **Budapest, on the River Danube.** *Buda and Pest were twin cities on either side of the River Danube. Now they have become Budapest, capital of Hungary. The river Danube is an important international waterway that flows through 9 countries.*

CAN YOU FIND THESE ON THE MAP?

- 4 seas (1 in the north; 3 in the south).
- A lake shared by 2 countries.
- A river with 4 lakes (these lakes have been made by dams).
- A river with a 3-letter name.
- A city with a 14-letter name.
- 2 capital cities very near the sea.
- A mountain over 2500 metres high (the highest part of the mountain ridge in the picture, right).
- A peninsula that is joined to the rest of Ukraine by a very narrow piece of land.

Estonia, Latvia and Lithuania are called 'the Baltic republics' because they lie alongside the coast of the Baltic Sea. Belarus ('White Russia') and little Moldova are landlocked countries, like several others on this map.

Ukraine is the largest country completely in Europe, but it is also one of the poorest. It has large areas of fertile farmland. Europe's largest coalfield is in the east, and there is iron ore for its steelworks. Crimea is now under the control of Russia.

▲ *The border of Poland (right) and Slovakia (left) runs along a high ridge of the Tatra Mountains. Can you find this border on the map below?*

37

ASIA

THE world's largest continent is Asia, which stretches from the cold Arctic Ocean in the north to the warm Indian Ocean in the south.

Mainland Asia nearly reaches the Equator in Malaysia. Several Asian islands are on the Equator: Sumatra, Borneo and Sulawesi. In the west, Asia reaches Europe and the Mediterranean, and in the east Asia reaches the Pacific Ocean. In the centre are the high, empty plateaus of Tibet and Mongolia, where winters are bitterly cold.

Two countries cover over half of Asia: Russia and China. India looks quite small – yet it is over ten times as big as Italy or the UK! But some of Asia's important countries are very small indeed, such as Lebanon and Israel in south-west Asia (Middle East); Singapore and Brunei in south-east Asia (Far East).

Over half the world's population lives in Asia. Seven of the world's 'top ten' most populated countries are here (see page 9). The coastal areas of south and east Asia are the most crowded parts. But people in these areas are in danger from typhoons or cyclones (also called hurricanes) and tsunamis (huge waves caused by earthquakes under the sea).

▲ *This Buddhist shrine is like many found in Nepal. It has been decorated with prayer flags and painted eyes.*

Height of the land

- over 6000 metres
- 4000 – 6000
- 2000 – 4000
- 1000 – 2000
- 400 – 1000
- 200 – 400
- 0 – 200 metres
- below sea level

sea level

▲ Highest point on the map

Scale 1:60 000 000

| 0 | 600 km | 1200 km | 1800 km | 2400 km | 3000 km |

1 cm on the map = 600 km on the ground

| 0 | 600 miles | 1200 miles | 1800 miles |

1 inch on the map = 960 miles on the ground

Turn to page which countries script here.

COPYRIGHT PHILIP'S

ASIA FACTS

AREA 44,387,000 sq km (including Asiatic Russia)

HIGHEST POINT Mount Everest (Nepal/China), 8850 metres (A world record as well as an Asian record.)

LOWEST POINT Shores of Dead Sea (Israel/Jordan), 400 metres below sea level (A world record as well as an Asian record.)

LONGEST RIVERS Yangtze (China), 6380 km; Yenisey (Russia), 5540 km

BIGGEST COUNTRY Russia, 17,075,400 sq km (A world record as well as an Asian record.)

SMALLEST COUNTRY The Maldives, 298 sq km

LARGEST LAKE Caspian Sea, 371,000 sq km (A world record as well as an Asian record.) The Caspian Sea is shared by five countries – which are they? (*Answers on page 97.*)

▲ **Himalayan Mountains, Nepal.** *The photograph shows Annapurna 1. Annapurna I is 8078 metres high and was first climbed in 1950. There are four other peaks in the group that are over 7500 metres high. The Himalayas are the world's highest mountain range, containing all the world's 'top ten' highest peaks, including Mount Everest.*

洲及港國灣

97 to find out are in Chinese

RUSSIA AND NEIGHBOURS

RUSSIA

AREA 17,075,400 sq km
POPULATION 142,123,000
MONEY Russian ruble

KAZAKHSTAN

AREA 2,724,900 sq km
POPULATION 18,745,000
MONEY Tenge

TURKMENISTAN

AREA 488,100 sq km
POPULATION 5,411,000
MONEY Manat

RUSSIA stretches across two continents, Europe and Asia. Most of the people live in the European part, west of the Ural Mountains. Some people have moved east to new towns in Siberia.

Because Russia is so huge, there are many different climates and almost all crops can be grown. The far north is snow-covered for most of the year (see page 88). Further south is the largest forest in the world – a vast area of coniferous trees stretching from the Baltic Sea to the Sea of Okhotsk in the far east. Grassy plains, called the steppes, are found south of the forest. In some parts, grain is grown on huge farms. Russia also has large deposits of many different minerals and can supply most of the needs of its many factories.

The republics of central Asia are mostly in a desert area – hot in summer but bitterly cold in winter. With irrigation, crops such as sugar-cane and cotton grow well. Space rockets are launched from the 'Cosmodrome' in the desert of Kazakhstan.

▲ **St Basil's cathedral, Moscow,** is at one end of Red Square. It is famous for its brightly coloured domes: each one is different. In the background are the domes and towers of buildings inside the Kremlin walls. 'Kremlin' means 'fortress'. The Moscow Kremlin has a cathedral and offices of the government of Russia.

▲ **In Uzbekistan,** people still use traditional looms like this one, for weaving silk, cotton and wool – but there is modern industry as well. Uzbekistan is one of the 15 countries created when the USSR broke up in 1991. Can you name them? (Page 37 will help; answers on page 97.)

THE ARAL SEA . . .

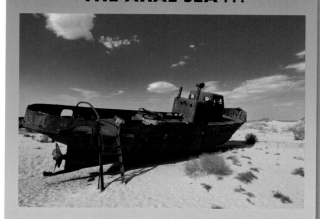

. . . is getting smaller. This ship was once in the Aral Sea, but is now on dry land. This salty lake is drying up because rivers do not refill it with enough water. The water is used to irrigate fields instead.

▲ **Siberia** has the world's largest forest. It stretches from the Ural Mountains to the far east of Russia. Most of the trees are conifers. They can survive the Siberian winters, which are long and extremely cold.

А	Б	В	Г	Д	Е	Ё	Ж	З	И	Й	К	Л	М	Н	О	П	Р	С	Т	У	Ф	Х	Ц	Ч	Ш	Щ	Ю	Я
A	B	V	G	D	E	YO	ZH	Z	I	Y	K	L	M	N	O	P	R	S	T	U	F	KH	TS	CH	SH	SHCH	YU	YA

▲ **The Cyrillic alphabet.** *Russian is written in the Cyrillic alphabet. This is partly based on Latin letters (the same as English letters) and partly on Greek letters (see page 35).*

The alphabet was invented centuries ago by St Cyril, so that the Russian church could show it was separate from both the Roman and the Greek churches. In Cyrillic, R is written P, and S is written C. So the Metro is written METPO.

CAN YOU UNDERSTAND THIS MESSAGE?

Use the key above: Х А Б А Р О В С К (square S4) is on the River А М У Р (see square S3 on the map). Now work out what the sign on the railway carriage (right) says. It is not as hard as it looks! Uzbekistan and some other republics of Central Asia are keeping the same language but changing their alphabet from Cyrillic to 'Latin' (as used in English and many other languages).

TRANS-SIBERIAN RAILWAY

DISTANCE (IN KM)	TOWN	TIME (IN MOSCOW)	DAY
0	Moscow	15:05	1
957	Kirov	04:00	2
1818	Yekaterinburg	16:25	2
2716	Omsk	03:13	3
3343	Novosibirsk	10:44	3
4104	Krasnoyarsk	22:31	3
5184	Irkutsk	16:23	4
5647	Ulan Ude	00:02	5
6204	Chita	09:23	5
7313	Skovorodino	05:20	6
8531	Khabarovsk	01:10	7
9297	Vladivostok	13:30*	7

It takes a week to cross Russia by train, and you must change your watch seven times. Here is the distance chart and timetable (only the main stops are shown).

МОСКВА–ВЛАДИВОСТОК

This is the plate on the side of the train. The translation is on page 97. This is one of the world's most exciting train journeys.

* This is 20:30 local time in Vladivostok.

At these stations, there is time for a quick walk – and some bartering. But don't forget to allow another week to come back!

Scale 1:45 000 000

1 cm on the map = 450 km on the ground

1 inch on the map = 720 miles on the ground

Height of the land

over 6000 metres
4000 – 6000
2000 – 4000
1000 – 2000
400 – 1000
200 – 400
0 – 200 metres
below sea level

▲ Highest point on the map

Country boundaries
Large cities
Moscow Capital cities underlined

MIDDLE EAST

▲ *Craft stall in San'a, Yemen. These men are making decorative daggers which are worn by men and older boys in Yemen. This small workshop opens directly off one of the narrow streets in the old part of San'a, the capital of Yemen. Craft industries still thrive in towns and villages all over the Middle East.*

SAUDI ARABIA

AREA 2,149,690 sq km
POPULATION 33,091,000
MONEY Saudi riyal

JORDAN

AREA 89,342 sq km
POPULATION 10,458,000
MONEY Jordan dinar

IRAN

AREA 1,648,195 sq km
POPULATION 83,025,000
MONEY Iranian rial

THE 'Middle East' is another name for 'south-west Asia'. It is the part of Asia which is closest to Europe and Africa. In fact, it is the only place where three continents meet. Turkey is partly in Europe and mostly in Asia. Of all the countries on this map, Turkey and Iran have the most people.

Most of the Middle East is semi-desert or desert. Yet many great civilizations have existed here, such as the Assyrian, the Babylonian and the Persian. Their monuments are found in the fertile valleys of the largest rivers, the Tigris and the Euphrates. During the fighting in Iraq, some historic buildings were destroyed and many people were killed.

Scarce water is used to irrigate crops in some places. In others, herds of sheep and goats are kept. Only camels can be kept in the driest desert areas. Dates from **Iraq** come from desert oases; oranges come from irrigated land in **Israel**. So much water is being taken from the River Jordan that the Dead Sea is getting smaller. Some countries make fresh water from salt water, but it is expensive.

IRAQ

AREA 438,317 sq km
POPULATION 40,194,000
MONEY Iraqi dinar

CONSTRUCTION

▲ **Progress in Qatar:** *is shown by the highways and high-rise office blocks being built with money from oil.*

▲ **Yemen:** *this is an ancient multi-storey building made of mud bricks and built on top of a cliff.*

HOLY CITIES OF THE MIDDLE EAST

Jerusalem: a Jewish boy's Bar Mitzvah ceremony at the West Wall ('Wailing Wall'). The huge stones (in the background, on the right) are all that remains of the Jewish temple. Jerusalem is a holy city for Jews, Christians and Muslims. People of all three religions live here and many pilgrims and tourists visit the city.

Mecca: crowds of pilgrims surround the Kaaba (the huge black stone, centre) inside the Great Mosque. Mecca is the holiest city of Islam as it is where the prophet Mohammed was born. Muslims try to come to worship here at least once in their lifetime. But wherever they are, they face towards Mecca when they pray.

The Middle East has changed dramatically in the last 60 years. Oil was found beneath the Arabian desert and around the Persian Gulf. It is pumped out from below the desert and mountains and even from under the sea. The demand for oil has grown in Europe and all over the world. The sale of oil has made some countries very rich, especially **Saudi Arabia**, **Kuwait** and **Qatar**. Often the rulers have benefited most, but they have also used the money to build schools, hospitals, roads and office blocks. The 'oil boom' has meant that many foreign workers have come to these countries to construct modern buildings like the ones in the photo of Dubai.

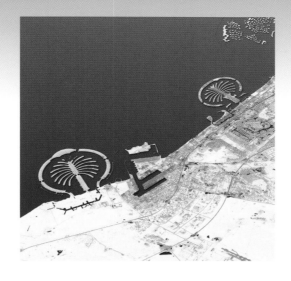

▲ *Dubai in the United Arab Emirates* is a modern city in the desert by the Persian Gulf. Man-made islands are being built in the shape of palm trees.

▲ *A camel in the desert of Jordan.* This boy is hoping tourists might want a ride in Wadi Rum, a dry valley in southern Jordan.

Scale 1:25 000 000

1 cm on the map = 250 km on the ground

1 inch on the map = 400 miles on the ground

CYPRUS
1:5 000 000

Under Turkish Administration
Nicosia
Limassol

THE HOLY LAND
1:4 000 000

Height of the land
over 6000 metres
4000 – 6000
2000 – 4000
1000 – 2000
400 – 1000
200 – 400
0 – 200 metres
below sea level
▲ Highest point on the map

Country boundaries
Large cities
Capital cities underlined
Tehran

COPYRIGHT PHILIP'S

SOUTH ASIA

AREA 3,287,263 sq km
POPULATION 1,296,834,000
MONEY Indian rupee
CAPITAL New Delhi

PAKISTAN

AREA 796,095 sq km
POPULATION 207,863,000
MONEY Pakistani rupee
CAPITAL Islamabad

SRI LANKA

AREA 65,610 sq km
POPULATION 22,409,000
MONEY Sri Lankan rupee

THE world's highest mountains appear on this map, including Mount Everest. The Himalayas form a great mountain chain which joins on to other high mountain areas, such as the Hindu Kush.

More than 1400 million people live in south Asia. The deserts and mountains do not have many people, but the river valleys, plains and plateaus are crowded.

Afghanistan, **Bhutan** and **Nepal** are rugged, mountainous countries.

Bangladesh is very different: it is mostly flat, low-lying land where the great rivers Ganges and Brahmaputra reach the sea.

Pakistan has very little rain, but the River Indus is used to irrigate crops.

India is the largest country. It stretches 3300 kilometres from the Himalayas to Cape Comorin. Most people live in the villages, but towns and cities are growing fast and are overcrowded. There are many modern factories, and India makes more films than any other country.

Sri Lanka (once called Ceylon) is a mountainous island off the coast of India.

The Maldives are a chain of low, flat, coral islands in the Indian Ocean.

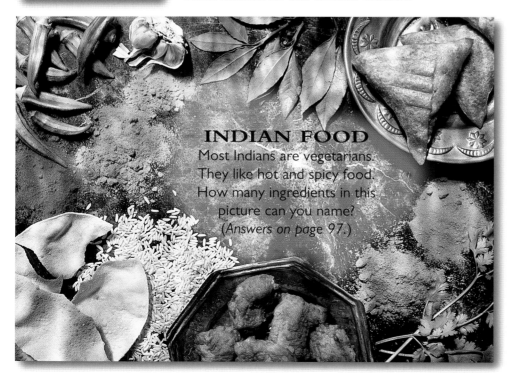

INDIAN FOOD
Most Indians are vegetarians. They like hot and spicy food. How many ingredients in this picture can you name? (*Answers on page 97.*)

▲ *Wool for carpets.* This lady in northern India is winding wool which will be used to make carpets. She sits in the courtyard of her house, where the ploughs and pots and pans are also kept.

TEA PLANTATIONS

Tea is an important crop in the hills of Sri Lanka where nights are cool, and there is plenty of rain. Women pick the new young leaves from the bushes (as shown on the stamp). The leaves are then dried and crushed, and packed into large tea chests for storage. 'Ceylon Tea' is one of Sri Lanka's most important exports. Where does the tea you drink come from?

AFGHANISTAN

AREA 652,090 sq km
POPULATION 34,941,000
MONEY Afghani

NEPAL

AREA 147,181 sq km
POPULATION 29,718,000
MONEY Nepalese rupee

Religion is very important in the lives of people in south Asia.

Hinduism is the oldest religion, and most people in India and Nepal are Hindus.

Buddhism began in India, but only Sri Lanka and Bhutan are mainly Buddhist today.

Islam is the religion of most people in Afghanistan, Pakistan and Bangladesh. There are many Muslims in India, too

Many **Sikhs** live in northern India; there are also **Christian** groups in all these countries.

Rice is an important food crop in south Asia. It grows best where the land is flat, and where the weather is hot and wet. In a good year, rice grows in the wet fields and is ready for harvesting after four or five months. If the monsoon fails and there is a drought, the seedlings will shrivel up; too much rain and the seedlings will drown. If the rice crop fails, many people go hungry. Where irrigation is available, the farmer can control the water supply and may be able to grow two rice crops a year.

▲ *These men are planting out rice seedlings in the wet soil.*

► **The Markhor** *is a rare goat with curled horns that lives in the mountains of Pakistan and Afghanistan.*

MOUNT EVEREST

Mount Everest is the world's highest mountain – 8850 metres above sea level. It was not climbed until 1953.

Everest is on the border of Nepal and Tibet (now part of China) – find it on the map in square D2. It is called 'Sagarmatha' in Nepalese, and in Chinese it is known as 'Qomolangma' (Queen of Mountains).

The photograph shows a glacier below the icy summit, and the bare rock that climbers have to cross. At this height, the air is very thin, so climbing is very hard and most climbers carry oxygen with them.

SOUTH-EAST ASIA

PHILIPPINES

AREA 300,000 sq km
POPULATION 105,893,000
MONEY Philippine peso

THAILAND

AREA 513,115 sq km
POPULATION 68,616,000
MONEY Baht

SINGAPORE

AREA 683 sq km
POPULATION 5,996,000
MONEY Singapore dollar

▲ **Singapore** *is the world's most crowded country. Most smaller old shops and houses have been replaced by new skyscrapers.*

THE Equator crosses South-east Asia, so it is always hot. Heavy tropical rainstorms are common. The mainland and most of the islands are very mountainous.

Indonesia is the biggest country, by both area and population. It used to be called the Dutch East Indies.

The Philippines is another large group of islands, south of China. They were Spanish until 1898.

Malaysia includes part of the mainland and most of northern Borneo.

Brunei is a very small but a very rich country on the island of Borneo.

Myanmar (Burma) was counted as part of British India. It became independent in 1948.

Vietnam, **Laos** and **Cambodia** were once called French Indo-China.

Thailand has always been independent, and has a king.

▲ **Rice terraces, Bali.** *Rice grows on terraces cut into the mountainside in Bali. Each terrace is sown and harvested by hand. Bali is a small island east of Java. Some people claim that it is the most beautiful island of Indonesia, and in all the world!*

GROWING RICE

1 **Ploughing**	4 **Weeding**	7 **Harvesting**
2 **Irrigation**	5 **Fertilizing**	8 **Drying**
3 **Transplanting**	6 **Spraying**	9 **Threshing**

Rice is the world's most important crop. The nine stages in growing rice are shown above. It is hot, hard work. Rice needs plenty of water as well as hot sunshine. New varieties of plants yield more rice, but they also need more fertilizer, more water and more care.

▲ **Floating market in Thailand.** *Farmers bring their fruit and vegetables by boat to a market at Damnoen Saduak, to the west of Bangkok. Fish are cooked on some of the boats and sold for lunch.*

The mountains of South-east Asia are covered with thick tropical forest (look at the stamp of Laos). Rare animals and plants live here, but they will not survive if the forest is cut down These areas are very difficult to reach and have few people. The large rivers are important routes inland. Their valleys and deltas are very crowded indeed.

Java, Bali and Singapore are among the most crowded islands in the world – yet several bigger islands, such as Sulawesi and Borneo, have very small populations.

▼ **Borneo** is a large island shared by 3 countries. Its forests are home to the rare Orang-utan.

▲ **Laos.** Elephants carry huge logs from the jungle. Laos was called Lanxang – 'land of a million elephants'.

▲ **Vietnam.** These young children are learning to draw a map of their country.

▲ **Indonesia** is mainly an Islamic country. The moon and star (seen here above a mosque) are traditional symbols of Islam.

Scale 1:25 000 000

1 cm on the map = 250 km on the ground

1 inch on the map = 400 miles on the ground

Height of the land
- over 6000 metres
- 4000 – 6000
- 2000 – 4000
- 1000 – 2000
- 400 – 1000
- 200 – 400
- 0 – 200 metres
- below sea level

▲ Highest point on the map

Country boundaries
Large cities
Bangkok Capital cities underlined

CHINA AND MONGOLIA

CHINA

AREA 9,596,961 sq km
POPULATION 1,384,689,000
MONEY Yuan

MONGOLIA

AREA 1,566,500 sq km
POPULATION 3,103,000
MONEY Tugrik

CHINA has over a billion people – more than any other country in the world. The map shows that there are many high mountains in China, such as the huge plateau of Tibet and the rugged mountains of the south-west where the Giant Pandas live. Not many people live in these mountains, nor in the deserts of the north, near Mongolia.

So the lower land of eastern China is very crowded indeed. Rice grows well south of the River Yangtze. North of the Yangtze, where the winters are colder, wheat and maize are important food crops, but it is hard to grow enough.

Taiwan is an island country which used to be called Formosa, or nationalist China. It is not communist and is not part of China.

Mongolia is a large desert country between Russia and China. Everywhere is more than 1000 metres above sea level. It is the emptiest country in the world, with an average of only 2 people for every square kilometre.

▲ **The Forbidden City** in Beijing was once the home of the emperors of China. Over 15 million people now visit it every year. Can you see the modern city in the distance?

▲ **Mongolia:** the Mongols were famous for their skill with bows and arrows. Today, archery is one of the main sports, along with horse-racing and wrestling.

▲ **Giant Pandas** live in the remote mountains in south-west China. Their main food is bamboo. This panda lives in a special reserve because a lot of the bamboo forests have been cut down to make more farmland.

▲ **The Great Wall of China** was over 5000 kilometres long (see map) – by far the longest man-made structure in the world. Building started 2000 years ago to keep China's enemies out. Notice the fortified towers.

This Chinese painting shows the amazing mountains of southern China. They are made of limestone and their strange shapes are real!

CHINESE NEW YEAR

This giant dragon is being carried in the New Year procession in Hong Kong. Chinese people all over the world celebrate New Year (or Spring Festival) in February.

▲ **Shanghai** *is a large city and important port of China. The skyscrapers are in the new Pudong area on the east bank of the Huangpu river. In the centre is the Oriental Pearl Tower.*

FACT BOX

- One out of every five people in the world is Chinese.
- The world's highest railway goes to Lhasa in Tibet, which is 3500 metres above sea level.
- The Chinese invented the compass, paper and printing.
- The Three Gorges Dam on the River Yangtze is the world's largest hydro-electric scheme.
- China is one of the world's biggest exporters of goods. What can you find that is 'Made in China'?

Height of the land

over 6000 metres
4000 – 6000
2000 – 4000
1000 – 2000
400 – 1000
200 – 400
0 – 200 metres
below sea level

▲ Highest point on the map

sea level

Country boundaries
Large cities
Beijing Capital cities underlined

Scale 1:25 000 000

0 250 km 500 km 750 km
1 cm on the map = 250 km on the ground

0 250 miles 500 miles
1 inch on the map = 400 miles on the ground

COPYRIGHT PHILIP'S

JAPAN AND KOREA

JAPAN

AREA 377,829 sq km
POPULATION 126,168,000
MONEY Yen
CAPITAL Tokyo
MAIN ISLAND Honshu

NORTH KOREA

AREA 120,538 sq km
POPULATION 25,381,000
MONEY North Korean won
CAPITAL Pyongyang

SOUTH KOREA

AREA 99,268 sq km
POPULATION 51,418,000
MONEY South Korean won
CAPITAL Seoul

JAPAN is quite a small country: it is smaller than France or Spain. But Japan has a big population – over twice as many people as France or Spain. Outside the big cities, most of Japan is still beautiful countryside.

This small country is mostly mountainous and many of the mountains are volcanoes. At school, children practise what to do when there is an earthquake, tsunami (a huge wave) or a volcanic eruption.

Japan has very few mines and hardly any oil, yet it has become well known for making electrical goods, cars and many other 'hi-tech' items that are sold all over the world.

▲ **A busy street in Kyoto.** *This city was the capital of Japan for over 1000 years – until 1868. It is famous for its cooking, its gardens and shrines. High mountains surround the city on three sides.*

▲ **Mount Fuji, beyond fields of tea.** *Mount Fuji (Fuji-san) is Japan's most famous mountain. It is an old volcano, 3776 metres high. Tea is important in Japan. It is usually drunk as 'green tea' and often with great ceremony.*

TEMPLES

▲ **Horyu Temple, at Nara, Japan.** The beautiful temple on the right is called a pagoda. Japanese pagodas are carefully preserved. Their unusual shape originally came partly from Indian temples and also partly from Chinese temples.

PUZZLE

▼ **Decorations for a Buddhist festival in South Korea.**
● What are they?
● What are they made of?
(*Answers on page 97.*)

▲ **Bullet train, or Shinkansen.** *Japan's 'bullet trains' go like a bullet from a gun! The trains run on new tracks with no sharp curves to slow them down. They provide a superb service except when there is an earthquake warning.*

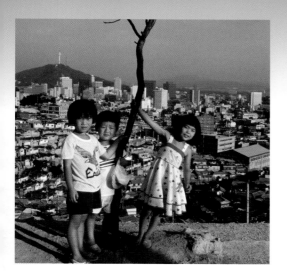

There are booming cities in the south of Japan, with highly skilled, hard-working people. Many of them live in the city suburbs and travel to work in overcrowded trains. Most Japanese families have small, space-saving homes. The main room is usually a living room by day, then the beds are unrolled for the night.

In southern Japan, rice is the main food crop. Some of the hillsides look like giant steps because they are terraced to make flat fields. But northern Japan has very cold winters.

Korea is sandwiched between China and Japan, and has often been ruled by one or other country. Since the end of the Korean War in 1953, it has been divided into two countries by a high fence that is well guarded. Find the border on the map.

North Korea is a communist country. It has lots of valuable minerals, but the people are poor.

South Korea is smaller but it has a lot more people. It has become rich and exports items such as ships, electronic goods, trainers and jeans.

▲ **South Korea.** Seoul has been the capital of Korea since 1392 – but is now only the capital of South Korea. These children are playing on one of the many hills in the city.

Scale 1:10 000 000

1 cm on the map = 100 km on the ground

1 inch on the map = 160 miles on the ground

Height of the land
- over 6000 metres
- 4000 – 6000
- 2000 – 4000
- 1000 – 2000
- 400 – 1000
- 200 – 400
- 0 – 200 metres
- below sea level

▲ Highest point on the map

Country boundaries
Large cities
Tokyo Capital cities underlined

AFRICA

MOST of the countries of Africa have quite small populations – except for Nigeria and Egypt. But everywhere the population is growing fast. It is difficult to provide enough schools and clinics for all the children and there are not enough good jobs.

Imagine travelling southwards across Africa, along the 20°E line of longitude. You start in **Libya**. Your first 1000 kilometres will be across the great Sahara Desert (where you must travel in winter) – sand, rock and the high rugged Tibesti Mountains. Then you reach thorn bushes, in the semi-desert Sahel area of **Chad**.

By 15°N you are into savanna – very long grass and scattered trees. You cross the country known as **CAR** for short. The land becomes greener and at about 5°N you reach the

equatorial rainforest ... a real jungle! You are now in **Congo**.

Then the same story happens in reverse – savanna in **Angola**; then semi-desert (the Kalahari and the Karoo). Now you come down to green fields, fruit trees and vines that are grown in the far south. Finally, you reach the coast at the Cape of Good Hope – a journey of nearly 8000 kilometres.

▲ **The grasslands of the Savanna** *provide grazing for large animals.*

▲ **Children in Ghana.** *Everywhere in Africa, there are lots of children. The fathers of these children are fishermen: in the background you can see nets drying and big dug-out canoes. The canoes are made from the huge trees of the rainforest, and can cope with big waves in the Gulf of Guinea.*

Height of the land

	over 6000 metres
	4000 – 6000
▲ Highest point on the map	2000 – 4000
	1000 – 2000
	400 – 1000
	200 – 400
	0 – 200 metres
sea level	below sea level

Scale 1:55 000 000

0   500 km   1000 km   1500 km   2000 km   2500 km

1 cm on the map = 550 km on the ground

0   500 miles   1000 miles   1500 miles

1 inch on the map = 870 miles on the ground

WHERE DO NAMES COME FROM

CHAD Named from Lake Chad

GAMBIA, NIGER, NIGERIA From big rivers

GHANA, BENIN, MALI Names of great empires in West Africa a long time ago

NAMIBIA From the Namib Desert

SIERRA LEONE 'Lion Mountain' (Portuguese)

SUDAN Named after the region south of the Sahara

TANZANIA From Tanganyika (the mainland) and the island of Zanzibar

▲ **The pyramids of Egypt** are tombs built by slaves over 4500 years ago. The picture shows the largest, which are at Giza, near Cairo. They are still the largest buildings in the whole of Africa. They are near the River Nile, in the Sahara Desert.

COINS OF AFRICA

All the 56 countries of Africa have their own banknotes and stamps. Most countries have coins as well. Pictures on the coins usually show something about the country. The 5 Bututs coin from the Gambia (above) shows a fine sailing ship. There is Arabic writing because many people are Muslims. The 10 Kobo coin from Nigeria (right) shows palm trees.

AFRICAN FACTS

AREA 30,319,000 sq km

HIGHEST POINT Mount Kilimanjaro (Tanzania), 5895 metres

LOWEST POINT Shores of Lake Assal (Djibouti), 155 metres below sea level

LONGEST RIVER Nile, 6695 km (also a world record)

LARGEST LAKE Lake Victoria (East Africa), 69,484 sq km

BIGGEST COUNTRY Algeria, 2,381,741 sq km

SMALLEST COUNTRIES Mainland: Gambia, 11,295 sq km; Islands: Seychelles, 455 sq km (see page 9)

NORTH AFRICA

TUNISIA

AREA 163,610 sq km
POPULATION 11,516,000
MONEY Tunisian dinar

MOROCCO

AREA 446,550 sq km
POPULATION 34,314,000
MONEY Moroccan dirham

MALI

AREA 1,240,192 sq km
POPULATION 18,430,000
MONEY CFA franc

MOST of North Africa is desert – but not all. The coastlines and mountains of north-west Africa get winter rain: good crops are grown and the coasts of Tunisia and Morocco are popular with tourists.

Most of these countries are Islamic. **Morocco** has the oldest university in the world: the Islamic University in Fez. **South Sudan** is the only country that is mainly Christian. It was part of **Sudan**, but became an independent country in 2011 after a long civil war.

People can live in the desert if there is water. Some modern settlements have been built deep in the desert where there are valuable minerals, and water is pumped from underground. These minerals are the main reason why some countries are richer than others. **Algeria** and **Libya** have plenty of oil beneath the desert.

South of the Sahara is the 'Sahel' – a large semi-desert area. Some years have good rains; some years very little rain. **Mali**, **Niger**, **Chad** and **South Sudan** are among the poorest nations in the world.

▲ **A market near Timbuktu, in Mali,** is a place to meet as well as to trade. People bring the goods they hope to sell in locally made baskets or in re-used cartons which they balance on their heads.

EGYPT

AREA 1,001,449 sq km
POPULATION 99,413,000
MONEY Egyptian pound

SUEZ CANAL

This old print shows the procession of ships through the Suez Canal at its opening in December 1869. The canal links the Mediterranean with the Red Sea (see map: G1). It was dug in 1859–69 by Arabs, organized by a Frenchman, Ferdinand de Lesseps. Before the canal opened, the route by sea from Europe to India and the Far East was around the whole of Africa.

▲ **Oasis near Lake Djerid, Tunisia.** Water is just below the ground, so date palms can grow well. But in the background, great sand dunes loom on the skyline. If they advance, they may cover the oasis and kill the crops.

▲ **Mosque in Morocco.** This tower is a minaret: part of an Islamic mosque. It is used to announce the times of prayer to all the village. The village is in the Ziz River valley, south of the Atlas Mountains of Morocco. Notice the flat roofs of the houses and the date palms.

Egypt is a desert country; its fertile land is 'the gift of the River Nile'. It has the biggest population of any North African country. Its capital, Cairo, is one of the biggest cities in the world. The River Nile brings water to the valley and delta. The land on either side of the Nile is carefully farmed using irrigation and is crowded with people. The rest of Egypt is almost empty. Find Cairo and the River Nile on the world population map on page 11 which shows the crowded and empty areas very clearly. The lack of rain has helped to preserve many of the monuments, palaces and tombs built by the ancient Egyptians. The pyramids at Giza, near Cairo, are about 4500 years old (page 53). They are the only one of the Seven Wonders of the ancient world still surviving.

THE SAHARA DESERT

The Sahara is the biggest desert in the world. It is over 9 million sq km in size. From west to east it is over 5000 km; from north to south it extends about 2000 km and it is still growing.

The hottest shade temperture recorded in Africa, 55°C, was in Kebili, Tunisia, in 1931.

The sunniest place in the world, over 4300 hours of sunshine per year, is in the eastern Sahara.

The highest sand dunes in the world, 430 metres high, are in central Algeria.

The longest river in the world is the River Nile, 6695 km long.

WEST AFRICA

NIGERIA

AREA 923,768 sq km
POPULATION 203,452,000
MONEY Naira

THE GAMBIA

AREA 11,295 sq km
POPULATION 2,093,000
MONEY Dalasi

COTE D'IVOIRE

AREA 322,463 sq km
POPULATION 26,261,000
MONEY CFA franc

THERE are lots of countries in West Africa. In the last 300 years, European countries grabbed parts of the coastline and later they took over the inland areas as well. Now, all the countries are independent, but still use the language of those who once ruled them. English, French, Spanish or Portuguese is spoken. Many Africans speak a European language as well as one or more African languages.

Nigeria is the largest and most important country in West Africa. It has over 180 million people – more than any other African country. About half the people are Muslims, the other half are mainly Christians. Although English is the official language, there are about 240 other languages in Nigeria!

In many parts of West Africa, there is rapid progress. Most children now go to primary school, and the main cities have television and airports. But many people are still very poor. Civil war has made poverty much worse in some countries – for example, in **Sierra Leone** and **Liberia**.

▲ **Village in Cameroon:** building houses with mud for the walls and tall grass for thatch. These materials are free and the homes are less hot than those with corrugated iron roofs.

LIBERIA

AREA 111,369 sq km
POPULATION 4,810,000
MONEY Liberian dollar

OIL IN NIGERIA

Nigeria pumps up lots of oil from under the delta of the River Niger. Oil has brought money for some people but pollution for others. The oil is used for fuel and chemicals. Nigeria also GROWS oil that is used in food, soaps and cosmetics. It is made from fruit that grows on palm trees - see the harvest picture on the next page.

▲ **Market day, Nigeria.** Red peppers for sale in Benin City, in southern Nigeria. Red peppers are very popular in West Africa – they give a strong flavour in cooking. Markets are important in both towns and villages throughout Africa.

▲ **Women pounding yams, Benin.** They use a large wooden bowl and long pestles (pounding sticks) to break up and mash the yams. These root crops are eaten at most meals. It is very hard work: much easier if it is shared! They are probably singing to help keep a rhythm for using the pestles. The baby will love this!

The southern part of West Africa, near the Equator, is forested. The tall trees are being felled for their hardwood. Many crops are grown in the forest area and sold overseas: cocoa (for chocolate-making); coffee, pineapples and bananas; rubber (for car and lorry tyres). The main food crops are root crops, such as cassava and yams.

Further north, the trees thin out and there is savanna. The tall grass with some trees is suitable for cattle farming. There are big herds of cattle, and beautiful leather goods are on sale in the markets. Cotton and groundnuts (peanuts) are grown in the savanna lands. The main food crops are grass-like: rice, maize and millet. In the far north of West Africa there is semi-desert called the Sahel. The Sahara is advancing southwards and Lake Chad has shrunk in size.

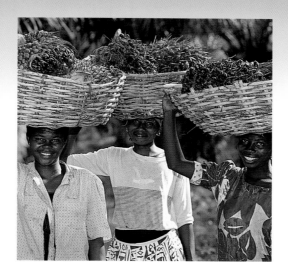

▲ **Palm-oil harvest, Ghana.** *These people are carrying heavy baskets full of oil-palm fruit. The oil palm grows in the hot, wet climate of the tropical forest. The fruits grow in bunches, with as many as 3000 bright-red palm fruits in a bunch. The fruit and the kernels are crushed in a factory to obtain oils. These oils are very useful for cooking and in making soap.*

▲ **Yeji ferry, Ghana.** *This big ferry carries lorries, cars, people and their heavy loads across Lake Volta. This man-made lake flooded Ghana's main road to the north. As the water rose in the new lake, the trees and much of the wildlife died. A fifteenth of all Ghana's land was 'lost' under the lake, and new villages had to be built.*

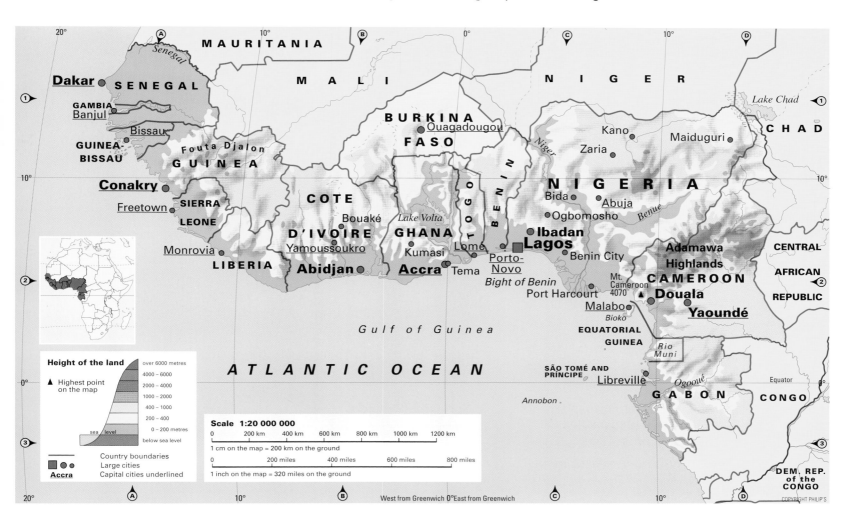

Height of the land
- over 6000 metres
- 4000 – 6000
- 2000 – 4000
- 1000 – 2000
- 400 – 1000
- 200 – 400
- 0 – 200 metres
- below sea level

▲ Highest point on the map

sea level

Country boundaries
Large cities
Capital cities underlined

Accra

Scale 1:20 000 000

0   200 km   400 km   600 km   800 km   1000 km   1200 km

1 cm on the map = 200 km on the ground

0   200 miles   400 miles   600 miles   800 miles

1 inch on the map = 320 miles on the ground

West from Greenwich 0° East from Greenwich

COPYRIGHT PHILIP'S

CENTRAL AND EAST AFRICA

KENYA

AREA 580,367 sq km
POPULATION 48,398,000
MONEY Kenyan shilling

ETHIOPIA

AREA 1,104,300 sq km
POPULATION 108,386,000
MONEY Birr

CONGO (DEM. REP.)

AREA 2,344,858 sq km
POPULATION 85,281,000
MONEY Congolese franc

CENTRAL Africa is mostly lowland, with magnificent trees in the equatorial rainforest near the River Congo. Some timber is used for buildings and canoes (see photograph right); some is exported. The cleared land can grow many tropical crops.

East Africa is mostly high savanna land with long grass, and scattered trees. Some parts are reserved for wild animals; in other parts, there are large farms for export crops such as coffee and tea. But in most of East Africa, the people keep cattle and grow crops for their own needs.

The **Somali Republic**, **Djibouti** and **Eritrea** are desert areas, but the mountain areas of **Ethiopia** get plenty of rain. If the rains fail, the crops fail and people go hungry. This part is sometimes called 'the Horn of Africa' because of its shape. Wars here have made the famines even worse.

In 1994 and 1995, a civil war in **Rwanda** led to a million deaths and more than a million refugees travelling to **Congo** and **Tanzania**. Wars like this damage people, the animals and the environment.

▲ **The River Congo at Mbandaka.** *Children who live near the river learn to paddle a dug-out canoe from an early age. The boats are hollowed out of a single tree with an axe. The River Congo is an important transport route. Mbandaka is a river port about four days by steamer from Kinshasa.*

FARMING IN EAST AFRICA

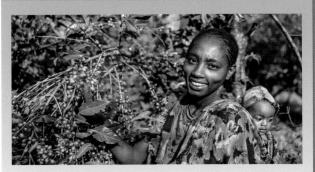

Picking coffee: Inside the cherry-like fruits are the beans that are dried, roasted and ground up to make coffee. This is an important 'cash crop' which farmers can sell. Other 'cash crops' are sisal (for making rope and sacks), cotton, tobacco and tea.

▲ **In a game reserve in Kenya,** *a group of zebra graze the savanna grassland. In the dry season, the grass is brown, but in the rainy season it is tall and green. The game reserves are carefully managed and people come from all over the world to see the wildlife.*

▲ **Gorillas in Rwanda.** *These gorillas live high up in the forested mountains. They are at risk as the trees are being cut down.*

▲ **Nairobi in Kenya** *started to be built in the 1890s as a railway depot and became the capital in 1901 – yet 120 years ago there was no town here.*

CENTRAL AND EAST AFRICA

In all these countries, there are many signs of development: new farm projects, new ports and roads, new clinics and schools. But there is much poverty, too, and people are moving to the cities and towns in the hope of finding work.

The population of this area is growing fast. It has doubled in less than 25 years. Some of these countries have the world's highest population growth rates, and more than half the population is young.

▲ **Mount Kilimanjaro, Tanzania**. *Africa's highest mountain is the beautiful cone of an old volcano. It is near the Equator, but high enough to have snow all year.*

Height of the land

▲ Highest point on the map

- over 6000 metres
- 4000 – 6000
- 2000 – 4000
- 1000 – 2000
- 400 – 1000
- 200 – 400
- 0 – 200 metres
- below sea level

sea level

Country boundaries
Large cities
Capital cities underlined

Nairobi

Scale 1:20 000 000

1 cm on the map = 200 km on the ground

1 inch on the map = 320 miles on the ground

ERITREA
○ **Asmara**

YEMEN

Red Sea

Blue Nile

SUDAN

Gulf of Aden

DJIBOUTI
○ Djibouti

Cape Guardafui

L. Tana

CHAD

Addis Ababa □

ETHIOPIA

Ethiopian Highlands

CAMEROON

SOUTH SUDAN

White Nile

Shibeli

CENTRAL AFRICAN REPUBLIC

Bangui

C o n g o

L. Turkana

SOMALI REPUBLIC

Ubangi

Congo

B a s i n

● Kisangani

L. Albert

L. Kyoga

Mogadishu

GABON

CONGO

Mbandaka

L. Edward

UGANDA
Kampala ○

KENYA

Kisumu

Tana

Equator

DEMOCRATIC

Lake

○ Kismayu

Pointe-Noire

REPUBLIC

Kigali

Victoria

□ **Nairobi**

INDIAN

Brazzaville

RWANDA

▲ Kilimanjaro 5895

□ **Kinshasa**

of the

Bukavu ●

Mwanza ●

Moshi ●

● Mombasa

OCEAN

Cabinda (Angola)

● Matadi

Kasai

Bujumbura

CONGO

● Kikwit

BURUNDI

Tabora ●

Tanga ●

Pemba

Lualaba

Kalemie ●

T A N Z A N I A

Kananga

● Mbuji-Mayi

Zanzibar

Dodoma

● **Dar es Salaam**

Lake Tanganyika

Kasai

L. Mweru

● Mbeya

ANGOLA

Likasi ●

MALAWI

Lubumbashi

COMOROS

Z A M B I A

MOZAMBIQUE

30° East from Greenwich

COPYRIGHT PHILIP'S

SOUTHERN AFRICA

ANGOLA

AREA 1,246,700 sq km
POPULATION 30,356,000
MONEY Kwanza

ZAMBIA

AREA 752,618 sq km
POPULATION 16,445,000
MONEY Zambian kwacha

SOUTH AFRICA

AREA 1,221,037 sq km
POPULATION 54,842,000
MONEY Rand

MOST of southern Africa is a high, flat plateau. The rivers cannot be used by ships because of big waterfalls like the Victoria Falls (see photograph right). But the rivers can be useful. Two huge dams have been built on the River Zambezi – at Kariba (in Zambia) and at Cahora Bassa (in Mozambique). The map shows the lakes behind each dam. The power of the falling water is used to make electricity.

Angola and **Mozambique** used to be Portuguese colonies, and Portuguese is still their official language – though many different African languages are spoken, too. Most of the other countries shown on the map have English as their official language.

Look at the map to find six countries of Southern Africa that have no coastline. It is more difficult and expensive for them to bring goods in and export their products. Railways and roads leading to ports in neighbouring countries are very important. **Zambia** has large copper mines and **Botswana** has the world's richest diamond mine.

▲ **The Victoria Falls from the air.** *The River Zambezi plunges over the falls into a narrow gorge. Africans call the falls Mosi-oa-tunya – 'the smoke that thunders'. They were named after the English Queen Victoria by the explorer David Livingstone. The falls are more than a kilometre wide and over 100 metres high. This is the border of Zimbabwe and Zambia, which are linked by the bridge at the bottom of the image.*

MOZAMBIQUE

AREA 801,590 sq km
POPULATION 27,234,000
MONEY Metical

▲ **Cape Town, South Africa.** *There are tall buildings in the city centre. The flat-topped mountain in the distance is 'Table Mountain'. It looks as flat as a table. When cloud covers it, it is called 'the tablecloth'. Cape Town is near the Cape of Good Hope, in the far south of Africa.*

A VILLAGE IN ZAMBIA

A Zambian girl drew this picture of her village during a lesson at her school. Her village is close to the River Zambezi in the west of Zambia. Look for a well, a man hoeing, a fisherman and a man looking after cattle. On the road there is a bus, a car and a van.

▲ **Ring-tailed Lemur, Madagascar.** *The island of Madagascar has wonderful forests and some of its wildlife is unique. But several species are under threat of extinction.*

The **Republic of South Africa** is the wealthiest country in Africa. The world's largest diamond was found here. It has the world's richest gold mine and the world's deepest mine. People rushed to the area around Johannesburg when gold was found in the 1880s. Now it is South Africa's largest city.

Most of the people are still very poor. For many years, black people were kept apart from the rich white people who used to rule the country. In 1994 they gained the vote and now they govern the country.

Namibia and **Botswana** are dry areas, with small numbers of people. Some of the rivers in this area never reach the sea. The map on this page shows big swamps and 'salt pans': these are the places where the river water evaporates.

Lesotho is a small mountainous country, completely surrounded by the Republic of South Africa.

Madagascar is the fourth largest island in the world. It is a long way from the rest of Africa. Most of its animals and plants are found nowhere else on Earth.

▲ *Children in Mozambique* hope for a better future. Their country is one of the poorest in Africa, and has also suffered from disastrous floods and drought.

Scale 1:20 000 000

1 cm on the map = 200 km on the ground

1 inch on the map = 320 miles on the ground

Height of the land
- over 6000 metres
- 4000 – 6000
- 2000 – 4000
- 1000 – 2000
- 400 – 1000
- 200 – 400
- 0 – 200 metres
- below sea level

▲ Highest point on the map

sea level

Country boundaries
Large cities
Capital cities underlined

COPYRIGHT PHILIP'S

South Africa has two joint capital cities: most of the government offices are in Pretoria, but the parliament meets in Cape Town. So both cities are underlined.

THE PACIFIC

Castaway Island is one of the 300 islands that are part of Fiji. This island with white sand beaches and coconut palms is surrounded by coral reefs.

THIS map shows half the world. Guess which place is furthest from a continent: it is to be found somewhere in the south Pacific. The Pacific Ocean also includes the deepest place in the world: the Mariana Trench (11,022 metres deep).

There are thousands of islands in the Pacific. Some are volcanic mountains, while many others are low, flat coral islands. Coral also grows around the volcanoes.

A few islands have valuable minerals – for example Bougainville (copper) and Nauru (phosphates). But some islands will disappear if the sea level rises.

INTERNATIONAL DATE LINE

Find this imaginary line on the map. When it is Sunday midday in London it is already Sunday evening in Australia and nearly *Monday* in New Zealand. But travel west and it is Sunday morning in the USA and *Sunday* is beginning in the Cook Islands. The date changes at the Date Line. Use a globe to help you understand why this is.

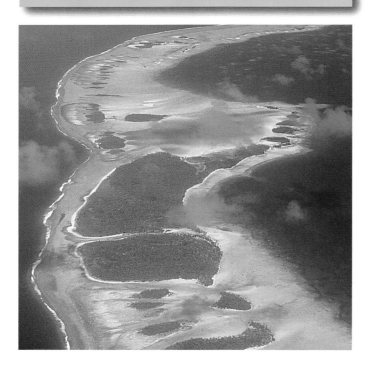

▲ *Coral reef in French Polynesia, from the air. Coral BELOW sea level is ALIVE! A reef is built up from the shells of dead coral. Gradually plants colonize parts of the reef.*

Most islanders are farmers. Many tropical food crops such as sweet potatoes, cassava and coconuts grow well; sugar-cane, bananas and pineapples are important exports. And, with so much sea, fishing is also important. Islands big enough for a full-sized airport, such as Fiji, the Samoan islands, Tahiti, and Hawaii (see page 72), now have tourists coming to enjoy the beautiful beaches.

▲ *Easter Island, South Pacific.* These huge stone sculptures each weigh about 50 tonnes! They were cut long ago with simple stone axes, and lifted with ropes and ramps – an amazing achievement for people who had no metal, no wheels and no machines. Look for Easter Island on the map (in square U11): it is one of the most remote places in the world. It is now owned by Chile, 3860 kilometres away in South America.

PACIFIC FACTS

OCEAN AREA 155,557,000 sq km – the world's biggest ocean

HIGHEST POINT Mount Wilhelm (Papua New Guinea), 4508 metres

LOWEST POINT ON LAND Lake Eyre (Australia), 16 metres below sea level

DEEPEST PART OF OCEAN Mariana Trench, 11,022 metres below surface. This is the deepest place on Earth.

LONGEST RIVER Murray–Darling (Australia), 3750 km

LARGEST LAKE Lake Eyre (Australia), 8900 sq km

BIGGEST COUNTRY Australia, 7,741,220 sq km

SMALLEST COUNTRY Nauru, 21 sq km

Most Pacific countries are large groups of small islands. Their boundaries are out at sea – just lines on a map. For example, Kiribati is 33 small coral atolls spread over 5,000,000 square kilometres of ocean.

AUSTRALIA

AUSTRALIA

AREA 7,741,220 sq km
POPULATION 23,470,000
MONEY Australian dollar

THE GREAT BARRIER REEF

The Great Barrier Reef is the world's largest living thing! It is an area of coral over 2000 kilometres long, which grows in the warm sea near the coast of Queensland. The reef is also home to colourful fish that swim among the coral. They can be seen from glass-bottomed boats.

AUSTRALIA is the world's largest island, but the world's smallest continent. It is the sixth-largest country in the world, smaller than the USA or Canada, but more than twice the size of India. Yet Australia's total population is small for such a large country. Most Australians are descended from people who came from Europe in the past 150 years.

Only a few people live in the mountains or in the outback – the enormous area of semi-desert and desert that makes up most of the country. The few outback people live on huge sheep and cattle farms, in mining towns, or on special reserves for the original Australians – the Aborigines. The north of Australia is tropical – and very hot.

▲ **Ayers Rock** rises steeply out of the dry plains in central Australia. It is 348 metres high. The sides have deep gullies and strange caves. For the Aborigines, it is a holy place called Uluru. Many tourists come for the hard climb or to watch the rock glow deep red at sunset.

▲ **The Flying Doctor Service** aeroplane is used to take people from remote areas to hospital, or to fly doctors to remote farms. People in the outback use 2-way radios to get medical advice and to keep in touch with one another.

▲ **Sydney Opera House** cost millions of dollars to build and has become the new symbol of Sydney. It is by the harbour, below the famous harbour bridge (in the background) which was built in Newcastle, UK!

AUSTRALIAN ANIMALS

Australia is not joined to any other continent. It has been a separate island for millions of years, and has developed its own unique wildlife. Most of the world's marsupials live in Australia.

The map shows that all the state capitals are on the coast. Canberra is a planned city built inland which became the national capital in 1927. Most Australians live near the coast and most live in towns. Sydney is by far the largest city. Yet much of the coast is almost uninhabited. The Great Divide separates the green coastal lowlands from the dry interior. The Nullarbor ('no tree') Plain is a desert by the sea.

TRICK QUESTION

Which was the biggest island in the world, before Australia was discovered? Think very carefully – then turn to page 97.

INDONESIA

Arafura Sea

PAPUA NEW GUINEA

TIMOR-LESTE

Melville I.

Timor Sea

Torres Strait

Cape York

INDIAN

Darwin

Arnhem Land

Cape Arnhem

Weipa

Cape York

Gulf of Carpentaria

Peninsula

PACIFIC

OCEAN

Wyndham

Kimberley Plateau

Barkly Tableland

Mitchell

Great Barrier Reef

Cairns

Coral Sea

OCEAN

Broome

Fitzroy

NORTHERN

Tanami Desert

Townsville

Great Sandy Desert

TERRITORY

Mount Isa

QUEENSLAND

North West Cape

Dampier

Hamersley Range

Macdonnell Ranges

Alice Springs

Tropic of Capricorn

Rockhampton

Great Divide

Newman

Gibson Desert

Ayers Rock (Uluru)

Simpson Desert

Barcoo

Bundaberg

Carnarvon

WESTERN

Musgrave Ranges

Charleville

AUSTRALIA

Great Victoria Desert

SOUTH

Kati Thanda-L. Eyre

Cooper Creek

Brisbane

Toowoomba

Gold Coast

Geraldton

AUSTRALIA

L. Torrens

Flinders Ranges

NEW SOUTH

Kalgoorlie-Boulder

Nullarbor Plain

L. Gairdner

Broken Hill

Darling

WALES

Great Divide

Perth

Fremantle

Darling Range

Whyalla

Port Pirie

Murray

Lachlan

Newcastle

Sydney

Cape Leeuwin

Albany

Great Australian Bight

Adelaide

Murrumbidgee

Wollongong

Canberra

Australian Alps

Mount Kosciuszko 2228

Kangaroo I.

VICTORIA

Geelong

Melbourne

Tasman Sea

SOUTHERN OCEAN

Bass Strait

Height of the land

▲ Highest point on the map

| over 6000 metres |
| 4000 – 6000 |
| 2000 – 4000 |
| 1000 – 2000 |
| 400 – 1000 |
| 200 – 400 |
| 0 – 200 metres |
| below sea level |

sea level

Launceston

TASMANIA

Hobart

South East Cape

Country boundaries
Large cities
Canberra Capital city underlined

Scale 1:20 000 000

0   200 km   400 km   600 km   800 km   1000 km   1200 km

1 cm on the map = 200 km on the ground

0   200 miles   400 miles   600 miles   800 miles

1 inch on the map = 320 miles on the ground

115° 120° 125° 130° 135° 140° 145° 150°

110° 115° 120° 125° 130° 135° 140° East from Greenwich 145° 150° 155°

COPYRIGHT PHILIP'S

NEW ZEALAND

THE ANTIPODES

New Zealand is on the opposite side of the Earth from Europe. This 'double map' is printed as if you were looking right through a transparent globe. It shows that the far north of New Zealand is at the same latitude as North Africa, and that the far south of New Zealand is at the same latitude as the centre of France. Now turn the map upside down!

THE two main islands that make up New Zealand are 2000 km east of Australia. Only 4 and a half million people live in the whole country. The capital is Wellington, near the centre of New Zealand, but the largest city is Auckland in the north.

The original inhabitants were the Maoris, but now they are only about 15 per cent of the population. Some place-names are Maori words, such as Rotorua, Whangarei and Wanganui.

South Island is the largest island, but has fewer people than North Island. There are more sheep than people! The Canterbury Plains are a very important farming area. Aoraki Mount Cook, the highest point in New Zealand, is in the spectacular Southern Alps. Tourists visit the far south to see the glaciers and fjords. The fast-flowing rivers are used for hydro-electricity.

▲ **Auckland** is sometimes called 'the city of sails' because so many people own or sail a yacht here. The city centre looks out over two huge natural harbours that are ideal for sailing. To the north is Waitemara Harbour and to the south is the shallow Manukau Harbour. Auckland is New Zealand's biggest city, and also an important port for huge container ships.

NEW ZEALAND

AREA 270,534 sq km
POPULATION 4,546,000
CURRENCY NZ dollar

KIWI FRUIT . . .

. . . were known as 'Chinese Gooseberries' until New Zealanders (nicknamed 'Kiwis') improved them, renamed them, and promoted them. Now they are a successful export crop for farmers, and many other countries also grow them – it is interesting to find out where YOUR kiwi fruit comes from.

▲ **This Maori boy** wears traditional war paint and beads. The Maoris lived in New Zealand before the Europeans came. Today, most live in North Island and many of their traditions have become part of New Zealand life.

▲ **The Southern Alps** stretch the length of South Island. The fine scenery attracts tourists, and the grassland is used for sheep-grazing.

North Island has a warmer climate than South Island. In some places you can see hot springs and boiling mud pools and there are also volcanoes. Fine trees and giant ferns grow in the forests, but much of the forest has been cleared for farming. Cattle are kept on the rich grasslands for meat and milk. Many different kinds of fruit grow well, including apples, kiwi fruit and pears, which are exported.

On the map below you can find: a sea and a bay named after the Dutch explorer Abel Tasman; a strait (sea channel) and a mountain named after the British explorer James Cook.

GEOTHERMAL POWER

Geothermal power station, north of Lake Taupo, North Island. In this volcanic area, there is very hot water underground. When drilled, it gushes out as steam. This can be piped to a power station (above) to generate electricity. Hot steam gushing out of a natural hole is called a geyser (below).

Height of the land

▲ Highest point on the map	over 6000 metres
	4000 – 6000
	2000 – 4000
	1000 – 2000
	400 – 1000
	200 – 400
sea level	0 – 200 metres
	below sea level

■ ● ∘ Large cities

Wellington Capital cities underlined

Scale 1:7 500 000

1 cm on the map = 75 km on the ground

1 inch on the map = 120 miles on the ground

COPYRIGHT PHILIP'S

NORTH AMERICA

NORTH America includes many Arctic islands, a huge mainland area (quite narrow in Central America) and the islands in the Caribbean Sea. The map shows the great mountain ranges, including the Rockies, which are the most impressive feature of this continent.

Almost all of the west is high and mountainous, yet Death Valley is *below* sea level. The rocks have been folded into mountain ranges, but the highest peaks are volcanoes. The Appalachian Mountains in the east are also fold mountains. In between are the Great Plains (known as the Prairies in Canada), which are flat and fertile. The Canadian Shield in the far north is made of very old hard rocks.

The political map of North America is quite a simple one. The boundary between **Canada** and the **USA** is mostly on exactly latitude 49°N. Look at the Great Lakes on both maps. Four of the five have one shore in Canada and one shore in the USA★.

Canada's two biggest cities, Toronto and Montreal, are south of the 49° line Find them on the map on page 71.

Greenland used to be a colony of Denmark, but now it is self-governing. Most of Greenland is covered by ice all year. See page 88 for more about Greenland and the Arctic Ocean, and page 73 for Alaska (which is part of the USA).
★ *Which lakes? Answer on page 97.*

▲ *Flyovers, Los Angeles, USA. There are three levels of road at this road junction in Los Angeles; sometimes there are traffic jams as well! In 1994, a huge earthquake destroyed many road bridges.*

Height of the land

▲ Highest point on the map

	over 6000 metres
	4000 – 6000
	2000 – 4000
	1000 – 2000
	400 – 1000
	200 – 400
	0 – 200 metres
sea level	below sea level

Icefield

Scale 1:50 000 000

0   500 km   1000 km   1500 km   2000 km   2500 km

1 cm on the map = 500 km on the ground

0   500 miles   1000 miles   1500 miles

1 inch on the map = 800 miles on the ground

Mexico and the seven countries of Central America have more complicated boundaries. Six of these countries have two coastlines. The map shows that one country has a coastline only on the Pacific Ocean, and one has a coastline only on the Caribbean Sea★. These countries are Spanish-speaking: in fact there are more Spanish speakers here than in Spain. Some of Mexico and all of Central America are tropical.

The **West Indies** are made up of islands. Some countries have lots of islands; some islands are one or two countries. They are shown in more detail on page 81. **Cuba** is the biggest island country. One island has TWO countries on it★. They are shown in more detail on page 81. This area is often called 'The Caribbean'. Some West Indians have emigrated to the USA, Britain and France.
★*Which ones? Answer on page 97.*

▲ *Market in St George's, Grenada.*
The West Indies have hot sunshine and plenty of rain. This is an ideal climate for growing vegetables and fruit. These stalls are stacked high with local produce. Many islands have volcanic soil which is rich in minerals and very fertile.

Grenada is an island country which grows and exports bananas and nutmeg. Find it on the map on page 81.

NORTH AMERICA FACTS

AREA 24,249,000 sq km

HIGHEST POINT Denali (Mt. McKinley) (Alaska), 6190 metres

LOWEST POINT Death Valley (California), 86 metres below sea level

LONGEST RIVERS
Red Rock–Missouri–Mississippi, 5970 km
Mackenzie–Peace, 4240 km

LARGEST LAKE Lake Superior*, 82,350 sq km

BIGGEST COUNTRY
Canada, 9,970,610 sq km

SMALLEST COUNTRY Grenada (West Indies), 344 sq km

RICHEST COUNTRY USA

POOREST COUNTRY Haiti

MOST CROWDED COUNTRY Barbados

LEAST CROWDED COUNTRY Canada

*The world's largest freshwater lake

CANADA

CANADA

AREA 9,970,610 sq km
POPULATION 35,882,000
MONEY Canadian dollar
CAPITAL Ottawa

▲ is
an air-picture of the prairies of central Canada. The huge flat fields of grain reach to the far horizon. Notice the tall buildings to store the grain.

▲ **In western Canada,** the Rocky Mountains are home to the large brown bears known as 'grizzlys'. The Rockies stretch for 4800 km through both Canada and the USA. They were a great barrier to the early explorers and to the early settlers, railway engineers and road builders.

ONLY one country in the world is bigger than Canada★, but 37 countries have more people than Canada. Most of Canada is almost empty. Some of the northern islands are uninhabited. Very few people live in the Northwest Territories, or in the western mountains, or near Hudson Bay. The farmland of the prairies (see the top stamp) is uncrowded too. So . . . where do Canadians live?

The answer is that more Canadians live in cities than in the countryside. The map shows where the biggest cities are – all of them are in the southern part of Canada, and none are as far north as Norway or Sweden in Europe. Toronto is on the same latitude as Venice and Milan.

These photographs show Canada in summer. In winter, it is very cold indeed in both central and northern Canada. Children go to school even when it is 40° below zero. The mildest winters are in the south-west, around Vancouver.

★ *Which country? See page 9.*

▲ **Quebec City.** The Chateau Frontenac (seen on the left) is built in the style of a French chateau (castle). This part of Canada was once owned by the French, and the people still speak French. On the right is the port beside the River St Lawrence. Large ocean-going ships can dock here.

▲ **The Niagara Falls** are between Lake Erie and Lake Ontario, on the border of the USA and Canada. One part is called the Horseshoe Falls: can you see why? Ships have to use a canal with locks to get past the falls. The falling water is used to generate hydro-electricity.

▲ **A long-distance train** travels through a pass in the Rocky Mountains. The trans-Canada railway helped to unite Canada as one country.

LANGUAGES IN CANADA

Canada has two official languages: French and English. So Canadian stamps say 'Postes/Postage', instead of only 'Postage'. Most of the French-speaking Canadians live in the province of Quebec, which once belonged to France. The biggest city in Quebec is Montreal: it is four times as big as Ottawa, the capital of Canada.

▲ **Vancouver, British Columbia:** *the biggest city in the west of Canada.*

Scale 1:25 000 000

| 0 | 250 km | 500 km | 750 km | 1000 km |

1 cm on the map = 250 km on the ground

| 0 | 250 miles | 500 miles |

1 inch on the map = 400 miles on the ground

Height of the land

over 6000 metres
4000 – 6000
2000 – 4000
1000 – 2000
400 – 1000
200 – 400
0 – 200 metres
sea level
below sea level

▲ Highest point on the map

Country boundaries
Province boundaries
Large cities
Ottawa Capital cities underlined

USA

WHO are 'the Americans'? Of every 100 people in the USA, over 80 have ancestors from Europe. The first colonists came from Britain, France and Spain, but later on, people came from almost all parts of Europe to the United States.

About 12 people out of every 100 came from West Africa, brought to the USA as slaves to work in the southern states. By 1865, the slaves were free. Many black Americans now live in the north-east. More recently, many Spanish-speaking people have arrived from Mexico and Puerto Rico.

There are now fewer than 1 million American Indians in the USA, some of whom live on special reservations.

▲ **American football** is a popular sport in the USA. Two teams of 11 people compete for points by trying to get the ball over their opponents' 'end zone'. Teams travel huge distances to compete with each other.

STARS AND STRIPES

In 1776 there were only 13 states in the USA: so the US flag had 13 stars and 13 stripes. As more and more states joined

the USA, more stars were added to the flag. Now there are 50 states, and 50 stars.

HAWAII

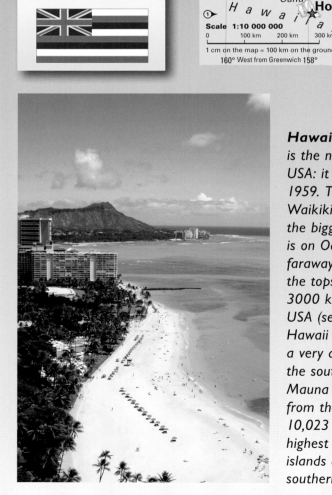

Hawaii

is the newest state in the USA: it became a state in 1959. The picture shows Waikiki beach in Honolulu, the biggest city. Honolulu is on Oahu island. These faraway Pacific islands are the tops of volcanoes, over 3000 km from mainland USA (see map page 63). Hawaii island itself has a very active volcano in the south. If the height of Mauna Kea is measured from the seabed, it is 10,023 metres: the world's highest mountain. The islands are the most southerly part of the USA.

▲ **The bald eagle** (above) is the USA's national bird. This bird of prey is unique to North America and can be found in Canada, Alaska, the USA and northern Mexico.

USA

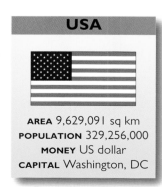

AREA 9,629,091 sq km
POPULATION 329,256,000
MONEY US dollar
CAPITAL Washington, DC

The maps show the 50 states of the USA. The first 13 states were on the east coast. They were settled by Europeans who had sailed across the Atlantic Ocean. As the Americans moved westwards, so more states were formed. The western states are bigger than the states in the east. You can see their straight boundaries on the map: those boundaries were drawn *before* the settlers arrived.

DISTANCE CHART

Read the chart just like a tables-chart, or a graph. The distance chart shows how big the USA is. How far is it from Seattle to Miami? Or from New Orleans to Chicago? (*Answers on page 97.*)

Road distances in km	New York	Miami	Chicago	New Orleans	Seattle
Miami	2138				
Chicago	1346	2198			
New Orleans	2131	1406	1488		
Seattle	4613	5445	3288	4211	
San Francisco	4850	4915	3499	3622	1352

ALASKA

Alaska is the biggest state of the USA – but has the fewest people. It was bought from Russia in 1867 for $7 million: the best bargain ever, particularly as oil was discovered a hundred years later. Oil has helped Alaska to become rich. Timber and fish are the other main products. Much of Alaska is mountainous or covered in forest. In the north, there is darkness all day in December, and months of ice-cold weather. But in the short summer, visitors love the long days and short nights. Farming is not possible in most of Alaska – except in the far south.

DID YOU KNOW? The Bering Strait is the only sea route from the Pacific to the Arctic Ocean, but it is often frozen over.

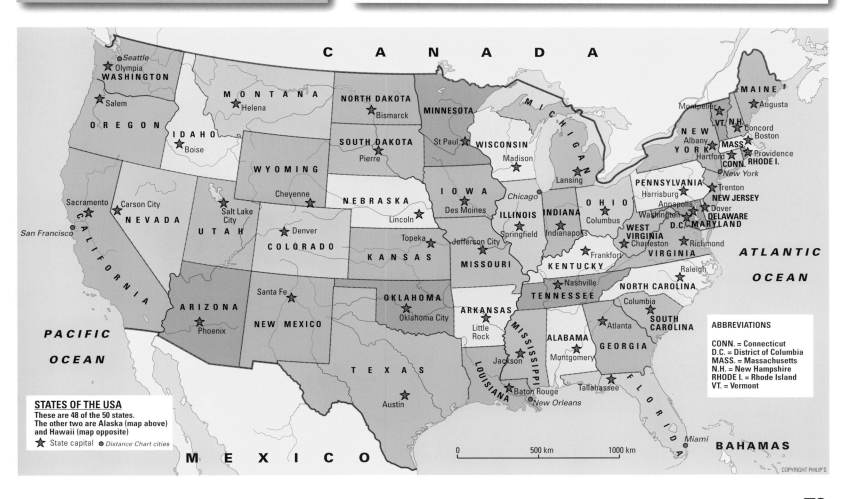

STATES OF THE USA
These are 48 of the 50 states.
The other two are Alaska (map above) and Hawaii (map opposite)
★ State capital ● Distance Chart cities

ABBREVIATIONS

CONN. = Connecticut
D.C. = District of Columbia
MASS. = Massachusetts
N.H. = New Hampshire
RHODE I. = Rhode Island
VT. = Vermont

EASTERN USA

NEW YORK

OHIO

MARYLAND

THE map shows only half the USA, but over three-quarters of the population live in this half of the country.

The great cities of the north-east were the first big industrial areas in America. Pittsburgh's American football team is still called the Pittsburgh Steelers, even though nearly all of the steelworks have closed down.

In recent years, many people have moved from the 'snow-belt' of the north to the 'sun-belt' of the south. New industries are booming in the south, where once there was much poverty. And many older people retire to Florida, where even midwinter feels almost like summer.

In the southern states it is hot enough for cotton, tobacco and peanuts to be successful crops. The palm tree on the flag of South Carolina (below, right) suggests that the climate of this part of America is nearly tropical. Summers are very hot and humid and winters are mostly mild. But hurricanes can cause serious flooding and damage near the coast.

The Appalachian Mountains are beautiful, especially in the autumn (fall), when the leaves turn red. But this area is the poorest part of the USA. Coal mines have closed and farmland is poor. The good farmland is west of the Appalachians, where you can drive for many kilometres past fields of wheat and sweetcorn.

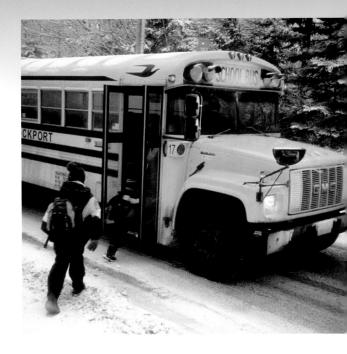

▲ **The school bus in New Hampshire.**
The north-east corner of the USA is called New England and was settled by English colonists. The settlers named their towns and villages after places they had known in England. This bus is taking the children to school in the snow!

WHICH US CITY IS MOST IMPORTANT?

Washington, DC, is the capital city, where the President lives. But New York has far more people and industries than Washington. So both are the most important city – but in different ways.

▲ **The Statue of Liberty** *stands on an island in New York harbour. When people arrived by ship, the statue was there to greet them! The torch at the top is 93 metres above the ground.*

▲ **Skyscrapers in Chicago,** *the biggest inland city in the USA. The world's first skyscraper was built here in 1885. These skyscrapers look out over Lake Michigan. The lake shore can freeze over in winter.*

TENNESSEE

S. CAROLINA

FLORIDA

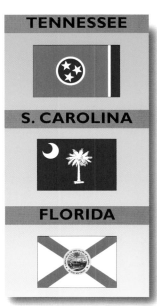

Every US state has its own flag: six state flags are shown on the page opposite. Several states were named after kings and queens of England – in the days when these states were English colonies. For example, North and South CAROLina use the Latin name for King Charles I; MARYland is named after his wife, Queen Mary, and GEORGia is named after King George II. But LOUISiana is named after King Louis XIV of France because France colonized a vast area along the Mississippi river. The map on page 73 shows the names of all the states.

GREAT LAKES

Try using the first letters of the Great Lakes to make a sentence:

Superior	**S**uper
Michigan	**M**an
Huron	**H**elps
Erie	**E**very
Ontario	**O**ne

If you remember these, you'll never forget the west-to-east order of the five Great Lakes!

THE MISSISSIPPI

The **Mississippi River** was known as the 'Great River Road' because it was an important route into the heart of the United State of America. 'Stern-wheeler' paddle-steamers travelled the river with cargoes. It is still an important river today. Dams (above) and locks make it easier for big barges to use the river. The dams also help to reduce the risk of floods.

▲ *The everglades of Florida* are an area of tropical wetlands. Lots of birds such as the snowy egret live here (see above). It is also home to more dangerous creatures such as alligators. Can you see the alligator? (Hint: look at the log under the water).

WESTERN USA

CALIFORNIA

COLORADO

SOUTH DAKOTA

MANY parts of the western USA have hardly any people. The Rocky Mountains are beautiful for holidays, but it is hard to make a living there.

The only big city on the high plateaus west of the Rockies is Salt Lake City, Utah, which was settled by the Mormons. Some former mining towns are now 'ghost towns': when the mines closed, all the people left. The toughest area of all is the desert land of Arizona in the south-west. The mountains and deserts were a great problem to the pioneers, but today the spectacular scenery and wildlife are preserved in large national parks.

▲ **The 'Wild West'.** Scenes like this one are rare now, except when they are put on for the many tourists who visit the area. But in the days of the 'Wild West', 100 years or more ago, the skills of cowboys were vital for rounding up the cattle that roamed over vast unfenced areas.

▲ **Wheat harvest, USA.** Huge combine harvesters move across a field of wheat. In the distance is the grain store. Up to 150 years ago, this land was covered in grass and grazed by buffaloes.

WHAT DO THE NAMES MEAN?

The Spanish were the first settlers in the western USA, and they have left us many Spanish names. Can you match the name and its meaning? (*Answers on page 97.*)

Amarillo (Texas)	The pass
Colorado	Yellow
El Paso (Texas)	The angels
Los Angeles	St Francis
San Jose	Coloured
San Francisco	St Joseph

ENERGY

Energy conservation. A great idea! But Americans use more energy than anyone else in the world.

WYOMING

ARIZONA

WASHINGTON

▲ **Grand Canyon, Arizona.** The Colorado River has cut a huge canyon 1½ kilometres deep and several kilometres wide in this desert area of the USA. The mountains slowly rose, while the river kept carving a deeper valley.

NEBRASKA

OKLAHOMA

TEXAS

The Great Plains east of the Rocky Mountains are flat but high. Denver is nick-named 'Mile High City'. All of the Great Plains were once grass. Where there is enough rain, they have been ploughed up for crops of wheat and sweetcorn (maize). In drier areas the grassland remains and there are enormous cattle ranches.

The Pacific coastlands of the north-west have plenty of rain and the climate is quite like north-west Europe. The mountains and valleys are thickly forested and timber is an important product. Seattle is on a sheltered inlet of the sea.

CALIFORNIA

California now has more people than any other state, and it is the USA's 'hi-tech' centre. It has many advantages. In the Central Valley, the climate is right for many crops: oranges from California are well known, and grapes grow well and are made into wine. The desert of the south is attractive to retired people – many people migrate here from all over the USA. But there is one big danger: earthquakes! So buildings have to be strengthened.

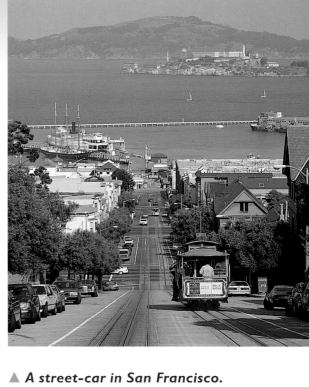

▲ **A street-car in San Francisco.** Street-cars still climb the steep hills in San Francisco, California. A moving cable runs beneath the street. The car is fixed to the cable and starts with a jerk! In the background you can see an inlet of the Pacific and Alcatraz – once a top-security prison island.

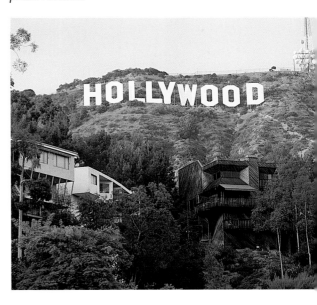

▲ **Hollywood** is a suburb of Los Angeles. Rich film-stars live here in expensive houses. The clear blue skies and lack of rain were helpful to film-makers. But now, Los Angeles has so many cars there is more smog from pollution than clear skies.

CENTRAL AMERICA

MEXICO

AREA 1,958,201 sq km
POPULATION 125,959,000
MONEY Mexican peso

GUATEMALA

AREA 108,889 sq km
POPULATION 16,581,000
MONEY Quetzal

PANAMA

AREA 75,517 sq km
POPULATION 3,801,000
MONEY Balboa

Mexico is by far the most important country on this map. Over 120 million people live in Mexico – more than in any country in Europe. Mexico City has a population of about 21 million: it is one of the biggest cities in the world. A major earthquake did much damage there in 1985.

Most Mexicans live on the high plateau of central Mexico. Industries are growing fast in Mexico City and near the border with the USA. There are very few people in the northern desert, in Lower California in the north-west, in the southern jungle, or in Yucatan in the east. But tourist resorts thrive on the Yucatan and Pacific coasts.

The other seven countries on this map are quite small. None of them has as many people as Mexico City! These countries were once ruled by Spain, but they have been independent since the 1820s. Civil wars have caused many problems in Central America. But the climate is good for growing many tropical crops, so lots of forest has been cut down for farmland.

▲ **Ruins at Chichen Itza, Mexico.** *Great temples were built by the people known as Mayas over a thousand years ago. These amazing ruins are in Yucatan, the most easterly part of Mexico. The tourists look tiny, which shows you how HUGE the pyramid is!*

BELIZE

AREA 22,966 sq km
POPULATION 386,000
MONEY Belize dollar

TORTILLAS – A RECIPE FOR YOU TO COOK

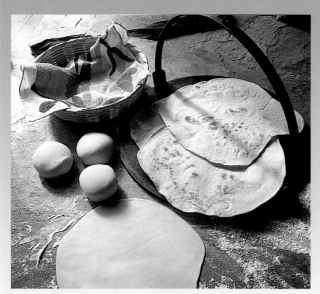

Ingredients: 225 grams of maize flour (sweetcorn flour); salt and water

1 Mix the maize flour, salt and water into a soft dough.
2 Pat into round shapes about ½ centimetre thick, and 12 centimetres across.
3 Melt a little margarine in a frying-pan.
4 Place the tortillas in the hot frying-pan.
5 For best results, turn the tortillas over.
6 Serve at once!

You have now cooked one of the most important meals of Central America. Maize (sweetcorn) was developed as a crop in the Americas, and is now grown in many parts of the world. You eat maize often as Corn Flakes and semolina.

▲ **The Toucan** *is sometimes called the 'banana-beak bird', for an obvious reason! It eats fruit and lives in the forest, nesting in a hole in a tree. If the forest is cleared, it will have nowhere to live.*

THE PANAMA CANAL

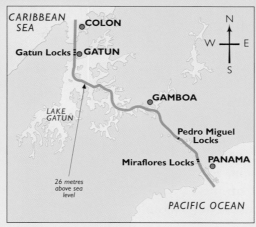

CARIBBEAN SEA
COLON
Gatun Locks • GATUN
LAKE GATUN
GAMBOA
Pedro Miguel Locks
Miraflores Locks • PANAMA
26 metres above sea level
PACIFIC OCEAN

N W E S

The Panama Canal links the Caribbean Sea with the Pacific Ocean. It was opened in 1914. Many workers died of fever while digging the canal through the jungle. It is 82 km long, and the deepest cutting is 82 metres deep – the world's biggest 'ditch'!

There are six locks along the route of the canal. The photograph (left) shows two ships travelling through the canal. The map and diagram show that part of the route is through Lake Gatun, at 26 metres above sea level. So the ships have to pass through three locks at each end.

Over 15,000 ships use the canal each year, and sometimes there are 'traffic jams' at the locks: it is the busiest big-ship canal in the world. Before the Panama Canal was built, the only sea route from the Pacific to the Atlantic was round South America.

In which direction are ships travelling from the Caribbean to the Pacific? Does this surprise you? Look at the map below.

PANAMA CANAL CROSS-SECTION

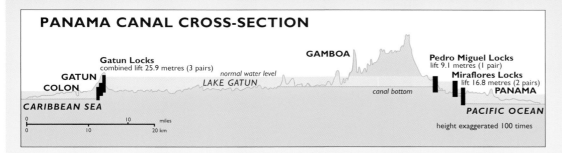

Gatun Locks
combined lift 25.9 metres (3 pairs)
normal water level
GATUN
COLON
LAKE GATUN
GAMBOA
canal bottom
Pedro Miguel Locks
lift 9.1 metres (1 pair)
Miraflores Locks
lift 16.8 metres (2 pairs)
PANAMA
CARIBBEAN SEA
PACIFIC OCEAN
height exaggerated 100 times

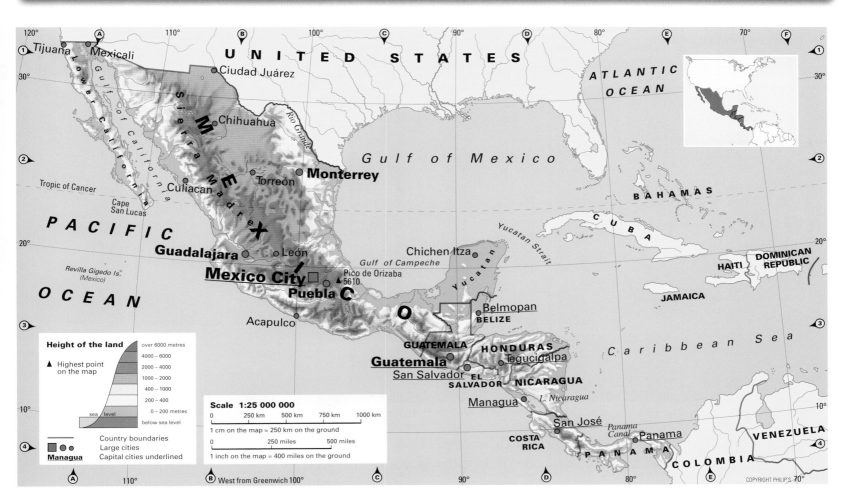

Height of the land

▲ Highest point on the map

over 6000 metres
4000 – 6000
2000 – 4000
1000 – 2000
400 – 1000
200 – 400
0 – 200 metres
sea level
below sea level

Country boundaries
Large cities
Managua Capital cities underlined

Scale 1:25 000 000
0   250 km   500 km   750 km   1000 km
1 cm on the map = 250 km on the ground
0   250 miles   500 miles
1 inch on the map = 400 miles on the ground

WEST INDIES

JAMAICA

AREA 10,991 sq km
POPULATION 2,812,000
MONEY Jamaican dollar

CUBA

AREA 110,861 sq km
POPULATION 11,116,000
MONEY Cuban peso

HAITI

AREA 27,750 sq km
POPULATION 10,788,000
MONEY Gourde

THE West Indies are a large group of islands in the Caribbean Sea. Some islands are high and volcanic, others are low coral islands – but all of them are beautiful. Most West Indians have African ancestors: they were brought from West Africa as slaves, to work in the sugar and tobacco fields. And in Trinidad, workers came from India as well.

Most of the islands are now independent countries – and tourism is more important than farming in many places. Cruises around the islands are popular. Winter is the best time to visit; summer is very hot and humid, with the risk of hurricanes.

In recent years, many West Indians have emigrated to the UK from Commonwealth islands, to France from Guadeloupe and Martinique, and to the USA from Puerto Rico. The most important crops for export are tobacco, sugar, bananas and special fruit such as nutmegs from Grenada. A few islands have developed their minerals, for example bauxite in Jamaica and oil in Trinidad.

▲ *Coconut palms and beach, Barbados.* *It is beautiful – but beware! The tropical sun can quickly burn your skin. And if you seek shade under the coconut palms, you might get hit by a big coconut! Even so, the West Indies are very popular with tourists – especially Americans escaping from cold winters.*

TOURISM – GOOD & BAD NEWS

Tourism is GOOD news because it brings money and jobs to many West Indian islands. The sunny weather means

tourists come all year. There is work in the hotels and restaurants. Farmers can sell more vegetables and a great variety of delicious fruit (left). Beautiful scenery is looked after so that tourists will come and visit – hot springs, waterfalls, old forts and churches as well

as coral reefs and lovely beaches. But tourism can also be BAD news ... pollution; noise; waste of water; and many local people do not want to be photographed by rich tourists who may not treat them as equals.

▲ *Dutch colonial houses, Curaçao. The island of Curaçao has been Dutch for many years. The colonists came from the Netherlands, and tried to build houses just like the ones at home. Several other small West Indian islands still have European connections.*

The flag of Jamaica (far left) has a meaning: GOLD stands for sunshine and natural resources; GREEN for farming and future hope; BLACK for hardships, past and present.

The West Indies used to be colonies of European countries. Today, most of the islands are independent, but still have close links with Europe.

Look at the map; can you spot*:
- An island that is part of the Netherlands?
- An island owned by the UK?
- An island that is part of France?
- A group of islands – half are owned by the UK; half by the USA?
- An island with two countries?
- The country with the most islands?

(* Answers on page 97.)

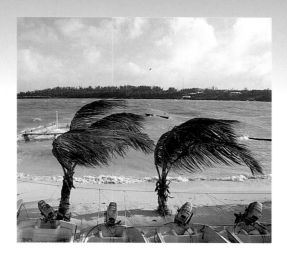

▲ **Beware of the hurricane season!**
What a contrast to the peaceful beach (see picture, left)! Violent tropical storms are a danger every summer. Strong winds can reach over 300 kilometres per hour, with torrential rain. They uproot trees and wreck boats and buildings; floods damage crops, roads and bridges.

▲ **Cleaning harvested bananas.**
These bananas have been grown in Guadeloupe. They have to be cleaned before they can be sold. Many people here depend on banana farming to make a living. The bananas travel to other countries in large refrigerated ships.

SOUTH AMERICA

A TOUR of South America would be very exciting. At the Equator are the hot steamy jungles of the Amazon lowlands. To the west comes the great climb up to the Andes Mountains – the world's longest mountain chain. The peaks are so high that even the volcanoes are snow-capped all year. Travellers on buses and trains are offered extra oxygen to breathe, because the air is so thin.

Squeezed between the Andes and the Pacific Ocean in Peru and northern Chile is the world's driest desert – the Atacama Desert, which stretches southwards from the border with Peru for nearly 1600 kilometres. Very few people live here.

Further south in Chile are more wet forests – but these forests are cool. The monkey-puzzle tree originates here. But eastwards, in Argentina, there is less rain and more grass. Cattle on the Pampas are rounded up by cowboys, and crops such as corn (maize) grow well. Further south is the very cold and dry area called Patagonia, where sheep farming is important.

▲ **Reed boats on Lake Titicaca,** the highest navigable lake in the world. It is high in the Andes, at 3811 metres above sea level. Totora reeds grow around the shores, and the Indians tie bundles of reeds together to make fishing boats. The picture shows the reed shelters they use while they make the boats and go fishing. In the background you can see a mountain rising from the plateau.

Lake Titicaca is shared between Peru and Bolivia. A steam-powered ferry boat travels the length of the lake.

Why is Lake Titicaca the only stretch of water available for the Bolivian navy? (Check the map!)

South America stretches further south than any other continent (apart from Antarctica). The cold and stormy tip of South America, Cape Horn, is only 1000 kilometres from Antarctica.

In every South American country, the population is growing fast. Most of the farmland is owned by a few rich people, and many people are desperately poor. Young people are leaving the countryside for the cities, which are growing fast. The city centres have skyscrapers, motorways and superstores, but most newcomers have to settle in the huge shanty towns at the edge of the cities.

ONE country occupies nearly half the total area of South America, and has over half the population of the whole continent: BRAZIL. Look at the map to see which countries touch Brazil. Which two do not?

▲ **Carnival in Rio de Janeiro, Brazil.**
Rio de Janeiro is the second-largest city of Brazil. Every year, it bursts into life and colour at carnival time, in February or March. Huge processions of decorated floats and dancers parade through the streets. Poor people from the shanty towns enjoy it as much as the rich people who pay for seats on the special stands.

SOUTH AMERICA FACTS

AREA 17,600,000 sq km

HIGHEST POINT Mount Aconcagua (Argentina), 6962 metres

LOWEST POINT Laguna del Carbón (Argentina), 2105 metres

LONGEST RIVER Amazon, 6450 km

LARGEST LAKE Lake Titicaca (Bolivia and Peru), 8300 sq km

BIGGEST COUNTRY Brazil, 8,514,215 sq km

SMALLEST COUNTRY Suriname*, 163,265 sq km

RICHEST COUNTRY Venezuela

POOREST COUNTRY Bolivia

MOST CROWDED COUNTRY Ecuador

LEAST CROWDED COUNTRY Guyana

HIGHEST WATERFALL Angel Falls, 979 metres (a world record)

* French Guiana is smaller, but it is not independent

TROPICAL SOUTH AMERICA

COLOMBIA

AREA 1,138,914 sq km
POPULATION 48,169,000
MONEY Colombian peso

ECUADOR

AREA 283,561 sq km
POPULATION 16,499,000
MONEY US dollar

BRAZIL

AREA 8,514,215 sq km
POPULATION 208,847,000
MONEY Real

BRAZIL is by far the biggest country in South America, and has more people (over 204 million) than the rest of South America put together.

Most people still live near the coast. Parts of the Amazon forest are now being settled, but large areas inland are still almost empty. The poorest parts are in the north-east, where the rains often fail, and in the shanty towns around the cities. Modern industry is growing very fast, but there are still too few jobs. **Brazil** has pioneered fuel made from sugar-cane for cars and trucks.

Colombia, **Ecuador**, **Peru** and **Bolivia** are known as the Andean states. Colombia is known for its coffee. Bananas and other tropical crops grow near the coast of Ecuador, but the capital city is high in the mountains. Peru relies on mountain rivers to bring water to the dry coastal area. Tourists come to see ancient Inca cities. Bolivia has the highest capital city in the world. It is the poorest country in South America: farming is difficult and even the tin mines hardly make a profit.

▲ **Machu Picchu, Peru,** the lost city of the Incas, is perched on a mountainside 2400 metres above sea level. The last Inca emperor probably lived here in 1580. The ruins were rediscovered in 1911.

PERU

AREA 1,285,216 sq km
POPULATION 31,331,000
MONEY New sol

▲ **Amazon jungle.** The hot, wet jungle covers thousands of kilometres. There is no cool season, and the forest is always green. The trees can be 50 metres high. New roads and villages, mines and dams are being built in the Brazilian jungle, and parts of the forest are being destroyed.

THE GALAPAGOS ISLANDS

These volcanic islands belong to Ecuador but are 1000 kilometres from the mainland. They have unique plants and animals because they have been isolated for so long.

The giant tortoises are the most famous and spectacular 'residents'.

▲ **Going to market, Peru.** This lady is a descendant of the Incas who lived in Peru before the Spanish arrived. She carries her baby on her back in a fine woven blanket. In most South American countries, the Indians are among the poorest people.

Venezuela is the richest country in South America because of its mineral wealth. Oil is pumped up from beneath Lake Maracaibo, and iron ore is mined from the plateau south of the River Orinoco. It also has coal, bauxite and gold. The world's highest waterfall, the Angel Falls, is in Venezuela.

In **Guyana** there are important deposits of bauxite, which is used to make aluminium. Guyana was once British Guiana, and **Suriname** was once Dutch Guiana. But **French Guiana** is *still* French.

DID YOU KNOW?

Ecuador means : the Equator (0°) crosses the country.

Colombia is named after Christopher Columbus, who sailed from Europe to the Americas in 1492.

Bolivia is named after Simon Bolivar, a hero of the country's war of independence in the 1820s.

La Paz, in Bolivia, means

▲ *Cattle and a cowboy in the Mato Grosso,* in Brazil. *This huge area of dry woodland and grassland is used to graze cattle. Horses are used to round them up.*

Height of the land
- over 6000 metres
- 4000 – 6000
- 2000 – 4000
- 1000 – 2000
- 400 – 1000
- 200 – 400
- 0 – 200 metres
- below sea level

▲ Highest point on the map

sea level

Country boundaries
Large cities
Capital cities underlined
Lima

Scale 1:30 000 000

0   300 km   600 km   900 km   1200 km   1500 km

1 cm on the map = 300 km on the ground

0   300 miles   600 miles   900 miles

1 inch on the map = 480 miles on the ground

COPYRIGHT PHILIP'S

85

TEMPERATE SOUTH AMERICA

ARGENTINA

AREA 2,780,400 sq km
POPULATION 44,694,000
MONEY Argentine peso

CHILE

AREA 756,626 sq km
POPULATION 17,925,000
MONEY Chilean peso

URUGUAY

AREA 175,016 sq km
POPULATION 3,369,000
MONEY Uruguayan peso

CHILE is 4300 kilometres long, but it is only about 200 kilometres wide, because it is sandwiched between the Andes and the Pacific.

In the north is the Atacama Desert, the driest in the world. In one place, there was no rain for 400 years! Fortunately, rivers from the Andes permit some irrigation. Chilean nitrates come from this area. Nitrates are salts in dried-up lakes; they are used to make fertilizers and explosives. Copper is mined high in the mountains.

In the centre, the climate is like the Mediterranean area and California, with hot dry summers and warm wet winters with westerly winds. This is a lovely climate, and most Chileans live in this area.

In the south, Chile is wet, windy and cool. Thick forests which include the Chilean pine (monkey-puzzle tree) cover the steep hills. The reason for these contrasts is the wind. It rains when westerly winds blow from the Pacific Ocean. These westerly winds blow all year in the south, but only in winter in the centre, and not at all in the north.

▲ **Geysers in the Andes, Chile.** *Hot steam hisses into the cold air, 4000 metres above sea level in the Andes of northern Chile. It shows there is still plenty of volcanic activity in the Andes.*

PARAGUAY

AREA 406,752 sq km
POPULATION 7,026,000
MONEY Guarani

THE ANDES

The Andes are over 7000 kilometres long, so they are the longest mountain range in the world. They stretch from Venezuela (page 85) to southern Chile. The Andes are fold mountains, with a very steep western side, and a gentler eastern side. Mount Aconcagua (6962 metres) is the highest mountain in South America. Many of the highest peaks in the Andes, such as Mount Guallatiri in northern Chile, are active volcanoes.

The higher you climb, the cooler it is. And the further you travel from the Equator, the cooler it is. Therefore, the snowline in southern Chile is much lower than in northern Chile, and in the far south glaciers reach the sea.

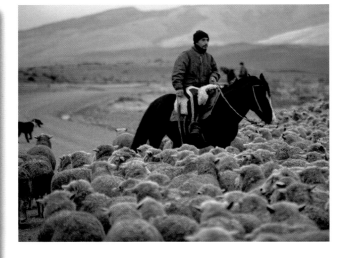

▲ **Sheep farming in Patagonia, Argentina.** *Southern Argentina has a cool, dry climate. Very few people live there – but lots of sheep roam the extensive grasslands. There are almost as many sheep in Argentina as there are people.*

The monkey-puzzle tree comes from Chile. Its proper name is the Chilean pine. The branches are a spiral of very sharp pointed leaves. The cones have tasty seeds. It was called 'monkey-puzzle' tree because to climb it would even puzzle a monkey!

Argentina is the world's eighth largest country. Its name means 'silvery' in Spanish: some of the early settlers came here to mine silver. But today, Argentina's most important product is cattle. Cool grasslands called the Pampas (see map below) are ideal for cattle-grazing.

Argentina is a varied country: the north-west is hot and dry, and the south is cold and dry. The frontier with Chile runs high along the top of the Andes.

Buenos Aires, the capital city, is the biggest city in South America; it has 13 million people. The name means 'good air', but petrol fumes have now polluted the air.

Paraguay and **Uruguay** are two countries with small populations: you can find the details near the flags on page 86. Nearly half the population of Uruguay lives in the capital city, Montevideo, which is on the coast. It is an important South American port. In contrast Paraguay is a landlocked country. Find its capital on the map. Animal farming is the most important occupation in both these countries.

All these four countries – Chile, Argentina, Paraguay and Uruguay – have Spanish as their official language. Most of the people have European ancestors, except in Paraguay where there are a lot of South American Indians.

THE FALKLAND ISLANDS

Port Stanley, capital of the Falkland Islands. The monument by the cathedral is a reminder of the whaling industry in the past. Today, fishing and sheep farming are important. These islands are a British colony in the South Atlantic with about 3000 people living there. They are about 480 km east of Argentina, which claims them as the Islas Malvinas.

▲ **Santiago, capital of Chile,** has a beautiful setting between the Andes and the coastal mountains. A third of Chile's people live in Santiago. Its name means 'St James' – the patron saint of Spain, which once ruled Chile.

THE ARCTIC

THE Arctic is an ocean surrounding the North Pole. It is frozen all through the winter and still has lots of ice in summer. It is surrounded by the northernmost areas of three continents, but Greenland is the only truly Arctic country.

For most of the year the land is snow-covered. For 4 months of summer the sun never sets; only then do temperatures creep above freezing. The snow and frozen topsoil melt, but the deeper soil is still frozen, so the land is very marshy. This treeless landscape is called the *tundra*. Reindeer and caribou can be herded or hunted, but farming is impossible.

In recent years, oil and other rich mineral deposits have been found. Canada, the USA and Russia have military bases near the Arctic Ocean.

From the Atlantic Ocean, there is easy access to the Arctic Ocean. But from the Pacific Ocean, the only route to the Arctic Ocean is the narrow Bering Strait, between Siberia (Russia) and Alaska (USA), which freezes in winter.

ARCTIC FACTS

Fifth largest **ocean** – 14,056,000 sq km;
World record for least sunshine;
Surrounded by cold **land**;
North Pole **first reached** in 1909;
At the North Pole all lines of longitude meet and every direction is **SOUTH**.

▲ *Inuit homes in Godhavn, on the west coast of Greenland. This village is called Qeqertarsuaq by the Inuit. In midsummer, most of the snow and ice has melted in this part of Greenland – but there is a big iceberg floating in the sea. These huge blocks of ice break off the ice-sheet that covers Greenland's mountains.*

▲ *Inuit (Eskimo) boy fishing for cod through a hole in the ice. Fish are a good source of protein for families in the far north. This boy lives in Nunavik in northern Canada.*

WILDLIFE IN GREENLAND

Land animals have to cope with very long winters. The Arctic fox turns white for camouflage.

ANTARCTICA

Antarctica is the continent surrounding the South Pole. It is the coldest, windiest and iciest place in the world! It is also very isolated, as the map shows.

No people live in Antarctica permanently. Scientists work in the research stations. Some are studying the effects of our climate warming up. Everything that is needed has to be brought in during the short summer. From November to January, icebreakers can reach the land, but huge icebergs are always a danger. In winter (from May to July) it is always dark, the sea is frozen, and people have to face extreme cold and dangerous blizzards.

No-one 'owns' Antarctica. The Antarctic Treaty ensures that the continent should only be used for scientific research. This means it should remain peaceful for ever. The flags of the 46 nations that have signed the treaty stand in a ring round the South Pole, near the USA's Amundsen-Scott base. Even Antarctica has more and more tourists visiting the area every year.

ANTARCTICA FACTS

Fifth largest **continent** – 14,100,000 sq km;
World record for coldest temperature;
Surrounded by cold **seas**;
South Pole **first reached** in 1911;
At the South Pole all lines of longitude meet and every direction is **NORTH**.

▲ **Rookery of Gentoo Penguins in Antarctica.** *Penguins cannot fly, but they can swim very well. The parents use their feet to protect the eggs and chicks from the cold ice! No land animals live in Antarctica, but the ocean is full of fish, which provide food for penguins, seals and whales.*

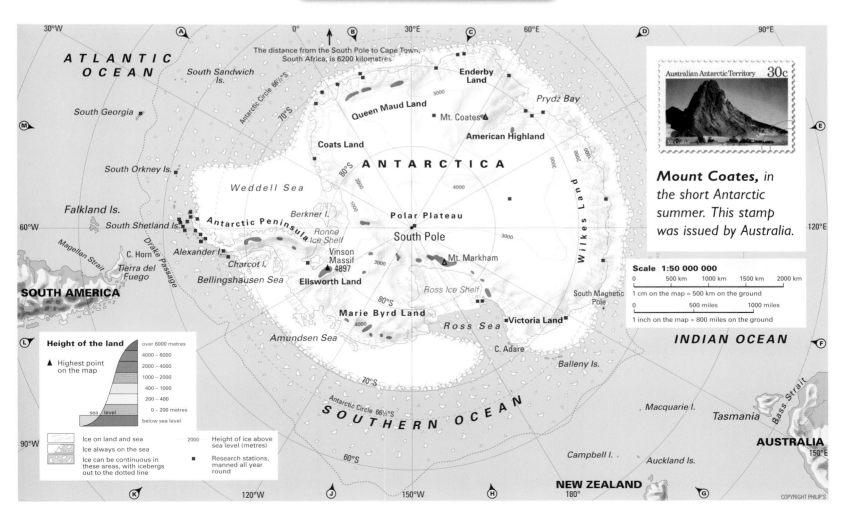

Mount Coates, in the short Antarctic summer. This stamp was issued by Australia.

Australian Antarctic Territory 30c
Mt Coates

Scale 1:50 000 000

0   500 km   1000 km   1500 km   2000 km

1 cm on the map = 500 km on the ground

0   500 miles   1000 miles

1 inch on the map = 800 miles on the ground

Height of the land
over 6000 metres
4000 – 6000
2000 – 4000
1000 – 2000
400 – 1000
200 – 400
0 – 200 metres
below sea level
sea level

▲ Highest point on the map

Ice on land and sea
Ice always on the sea
Ice can be continuous in these areas, with icebergs out to the dotted line
2000 Height of ice above sea level (metres)
■ Research stations, manned all year round

ATLANTIC OCEAN
South Sandwich Is.
South Georgia
South Orkney Is.
Falkland Is.
South Shetland Is.
C. Horn
Magellan Strait
Tierra del Fuego
Drake Passage
Alexander I.
Charcot I.
Bellingshausen Sea
SOUTH AMERICA

The distance from the South Pole to Cape Town, South Africa, is 6200 kilometres
Antarctic Circle 66½°S
70°S
Queen Maud Land
Coats Land
Weddell Sea
Berkner I.
Ronne Ice Shelf
Antarctic Peninsula
Vinson Massif ▲ 4897
Ellsworth Land
Marie Byrd Land
Amundsen Sea

Enderby Land
Prydz Bay
Mt. Coates △
American Highland
80°S
ANTARCTICA
Polar Plateau
South Pole
4000
3000
Mt. Markham △
Ross Ice Shelf
Ross Sea
Victoria Land
C. Adare
Balleny Is.
Wilkes Land
South Magnetic Pole
INDIAN OCEAN

70°S
Antarctic Circle 66½°S
60°S
SOUTHERN OCEAN
Macquarie I.
Tasmania
Bass Strait
AUSTRALIA
Campbell I.
Auckland Is.
NEW ZEALAND

QUIZ QUESTIONS

NAME THE COUNTRY

There is a long, thin country in almost every continent. Can you name the countries shown here – and name the continent in which they are found? (If you need help, look at pages 8–9 for a map of the countries of the world.)

NAME THE ISLAND

The name of the continent where each island is found is marked on each outline. Do you know (a) the name of each island, and (b) to which country each island belongs (or are they island countries)?

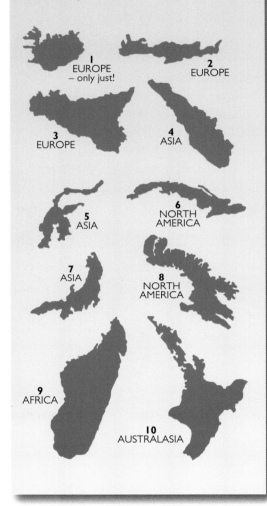

A MYSTERY MESSAGE

Use the map of the countries of the world on pages 8–9 to decode this message. Each missing word is all or part of the name of a country. (For some answers, letters have to be taken out of or added to the name of the country.)

I was _ _ _ _ a _ _ (east of Austria), so I bought a large _ _ _ _ _ _ (east of Greece), some _ _ _ _ _ _ ns (east of Norway) and a bottle of _ _ _ _ ugal (west of Spain). Finally, I ate an _ _ _ land (west of Norway) -cream. I enjoyed my _ e _ _ i (east of Mauritania), but afterwards I began to _ _ _ _ earia (south of Romania) and I got a bad S _ _ _ _ (south of France). A O _ _ _ (east of Saudi Arabia) told me: 'Just eat Philip _ _ _ _ sapples (south of Taiwan) and _ _ gypt (east of Libya), cooked in a Ja _ _ _ (east of Korea). Tomorrow you can eat a Ghban _ _ _ (east of Cote d'Ivoire) and some _ _ _ _ _ _ (east of Peru) nuts. It shouldn't _ _ _ _ a Rica (west of Panama) you too much.' I said: 'You must be _ _ _ agascar (east of Mozambique)! I think I've got _ _ _ _ ysr _ _ (north of Indonesia). I'll have _ _ / _ _ (west of Benin) to a doctor quickly, otherwise I'll soon be _ _ _ _ Sea (lake between Israel and Jordan).'

Happily, the doctor _ _ bared (island country south of USA) me, so I am still M _ _ d _ _ _ s (islands west of Sri Lanka) today!

GREAT RIVERS OF EUROPE

Use pages 18–37 to discover which great river flows through or near each pair of cities.
1 Vienna (Austria) and Budapest (Hungary)
2 Rotterdam (Netherlands) and Bonn (Germany)
3 Avignon (France) and Lyons (France)
4 Worcester (England) and Gloucester (England)
5 Toledo (Spain) and Lisbon (Portugal)

PLACES IN ASIA

Move the letters to find:
Countries RAIN; CHAIN; MOAN; AWAIT N; PLANE
Capital cities ANIMAL; DIARY H; THE TANKS; A BULK; COOL MOB

FIND THE COLOUR

Each answer is a colour. Use the atlas index and the maps to help you. Cover the right-hand column with a piece of paper and try to answer the left-hand column only. Award yourself 2 points for each correct answer to the left-hand column only, or 1 point if you used the clues in both columns.

1 A sea between Egypt and Saudi Arabia . . .

2 A big island east of Canada . . .

3 The sea between Turkey and Ukraine . . .

4 The sea between Korea and China . . .

5 The sea on which Arkhangelsk lies, in Russia . . .

6 A town in southern France which is also a fruit . . .

7 The tributary of the River Nile that flows from Ethiopia to Khartoum (Sudan) . . .

. . . and the river on the border of Oklahoma and Texas, USA.

. . . and a bay on the west side of Lake Michigan, USA.

. . . and a forest in Germany.

. . . and a (stony) river in Wyoming, USA.

. . . and the river flowing north from Lake Victoria to Khartoum (Sudan).

. . . and the river which makes the border between South Africa and Namibia.

. . . and a mountain ridge in eastern USA.

OCEANS AND SEAS

What ocean would you cross on an aeroplane journey . . .

1 From Australia to the USA?
2 From Brazil to South Africa?
3 From Canada to Russia?
4 From Madagascar to Indonesia?
5 From Mexico to Portugal?

What sea would you cross on an aeroplane journey . . .

6 From Saudi Arabia to Egypt?
7 From Korea to Japan?
8 From Denmark to the UK?
9 From Vietnam to the Philippines?
10 From Cuba to Colombia?

THINGS TO DO

COLLECT STAMPS WITH A THEME
A stamp collection soon grows. Try a thematic collection: choose a theme (topic) and collect stamps on that theme. For example, you could collect:
Holidays on stamps – such as the stamps on page 80.
Map stamps – small islands often issue map stamps to show everyone where they are!
Traditional crafts on stamps.

COLLECT YOUR OWN COINS
Ask people who have been abroad for any foreign coins they do not want – you will have an instant collection! If you cannot have the coins to keep, you could make pencil or crayon rubbings on thin paper. The coin box on page 16 is a good starting-point for making sense of the coins in your collection: each coin has a date, a value and a picture.

USA STATES QUIZ

All the answers can be found on the maps on pages 68–69 and 72–77.
* *Do NOT include Alaska and Hawaii.*

1 Which is the *biggest* state?*
2 Which is the *smallest* state?
3 Which state reaches furthest *north*? (Careful!)*
4 Which state reaches furthest *south*?*
5 Which state reaches furthest *west*?*
6 Which state reaches furthest *east*?
7 Which state is split into two by a lake?
8 Which state is split into two by an inlet of the sea?
9 Which two states are perfect rectangles in shape?
10 Which state is shaped like a saucepan?
11 In which state will you be if you visit Lake Huron?
12 In which state will you be if you visit Lake Ontario?
13 In which state will you be if you visit the Great Salt Lake?
14 In which state will you be if you visit the Mississippi delta?
15 Which state in *northern* USA is called South . . . . . ?
16 Which state in *southern* USA is called North . . . . . ?
17 There is only one place in the USA where four states meet: which states?
18 How many states have a border with Mexico?
19 How many states have a coastline on the Pacific?*
20 How many states have a coastline on the Gulf of Mexico?

ANSWERS TO ALL QUIZ QUESTIONS ARE ON PAGE 97

INDEX

HOW TO USE THIS INDEX

The first number given after each name or topic is the page number; then a letter and another number tell you which square of the map you should look at.

For example, Abidjan is in square B2 on page 57. Find B at the top or the bottom of the map on page 57 and put a finger on it. Put another finger on the number 2 at the side of the map. Move your fingers in from the edge of the map and they will meet in square B2. Abidjan will now be easy to find. It is the capital city of the Ivory Coast, a country in West Africa.

Town names are indexed to the square in which the town symbol falls. However, if the name of a physical feature goes through more than one square, the square given in the index is the one in which the biggest part of the name falls.

Names like Gulf of Mexico and Cape Horn are in the Index as 'Mexico, Gulf of' and 'Horn, Cape'.

Barrow, Cape	73	C1	Bournemouth	23	E5	Cape Town	61	A4
Basle	33	A1	Bradford	23	F4	Cape York		
Basque Provinces	31	D2	Brahmaputra,			Peninsula	65	H2
Basra	43	D2	River	49	C4	Caracas	85	D1
Bass Strait	65	J7	Brasilia	85	F4	Carcassonne	27	F5
Bastia	33	B3	Brasov	35	D1	Cardiff	23	E5
Bathurst, Cape	71	F2	Bratislava	37	C3	Caribbean Sea	81	C4
Baton Rouge	75	B3	Brazil	85	E3	Carletonville	61	B3
Bavaria	29	D4	Brazilian Highlands	85	F4	Carlisle	23	E3
Bayonne	27	D5	Brazzaville	59	A3	Caroline Islands	62	J8
Beaufort Sea	71	D2	Bremen	29	C2	Carpathians	37	D3
Beersheba	43	L9	Brescia	33	C2	Carpentaria,		
Beijing	49	E3	Brest	27	B2	Gulf of	65	G2
Beira	61	C2	Bridgetown	81	G4	Cartagena	31	E5
Beirut	43	C2	Brighton	23	F5	Carthage	55	E1
Belarus	37	E2	Brindisi	33	F4	Casablanca	55	C1
Belem	85	F3	Brisbane	65	K5	Cascade Range	77	A2
Belfast	23	D3	Bristol	23	E5	Casper	77	C2
Belgium	25	C4	British Columbia	71	F4	Caspian Sea	38	J4
Belgrade	35	C2	British Isles	23	E4	Castellon	31	F4
Belize	79	D3	Brittany	27	C2	Catalonia	31	F3
Bellingshausen			Brno	37	C3	Catania	33	E6
Sea	89	L	Broken Hill	65	H6	Caucasus		
Belmopan	79	D3	Brooks Range	73	B4	Mountains	41	H4
Belo Horizonte	85	F4	Broome	65	D3	Cayenne	85	E2
Ben Nevis	23	D2	Bruges	25	B3	Cebu	47	D2
Benelux	24–25		Brunei	47	C3	Celebes	47	D4
Bengal, Bay of	38	M7	Brunswick	29	D2	Celebes Sea	47	D3
Bengaluru	45	C3	Brussels	25	C4	Central African		
Benghazi	55	F1	Bucharest	35	D2	Republic	59	B2
Benin	57	C2	Budapest	37	C3	Central America	68	K7
Benin, Bight of	57	C2	Buenos Aires	87	C3	Ceram	47	D4
Benue, River	57	C2	Buffalo	75	D2	Ceuta	31	C6
Bergen	21	B3	Bug, River	37	F3	Cevennes	27	F4
Bering Sea	62	L3	Bujumbura	59	B3	Chad	55	E4
Bering Strait	88	A	Bukavu	59	B3	Chad, Lake	55	E3
Berkner Island	89	M	Bulawayo	61	B3	Champagne	27	G2
Berlin	29	E2	Bulgaria	35	C2	Chang Jiang,		
Bermuda	69	N5	Bundaberg	65	K4	River	49	E3
Bern	33	A1	Burgas	35	D2	Changchun	49	F2
Besancon	27	H3	Burgos	31	D2	Changsha	49	E4
Bethlehem	43	M9	Burgundy	27	G3	Channel Islands	27	C2
Bhutan	45	E2	Burkina Faso	57	B1	Chari, River	55	E3
Bida	57	C2	Burma = Myanmar	47	A1	Charleroi	25	C4
Bielefeld	29	C2	Burundi	59	C3	Charleston	75	C3
Big Timber	77	B2	Busan	51	B3	Charleville	65	J5
Bilbao	31	D2				Charlotte	75	C3
Billings	77	C2				Chartres	27	E2
Bioko	57	C2				Chatham Islands	62	M13
Birmingham			**C**			Chattanooga	75	C3
(UK)	23	F4	Cabinda	59	A3	Chelyabinsk	41	K3
Birmingham			Caceres	31	B4	Chemnitz	29	E3
(USA)	75	C3	Cadiz	31	B5	Chengdu	49	D3
Biscay, Bay of	18	G5	Cadiz, Gulf of	31	B5	Chennai	45	D3
Bishkek	41	L4	Caen	27	D2	Cherbourg	27	D2
Bissau	57	A1	Cagliari	33	B5	Chernobyl	37	F2
Bitola	35	C2	Cahora Bassa Dam	61	C2	Chiang Mai	47	A2
Black Forest	29	C4	Caicos Islands	81	D2	Chicago	75	B2
Black Hills	77	C2	Cairns	65	J3	Chichen Itza	79	D2
Black Sea	18	P6	Cairo	55	G1	Chidley, Cape	71	M3
Blanc, Mont	27	H4	Calais	27	F1	Chile	87	B3
Blantyre	61	C2	Calcutta =			China	49	C3
Blenheim	67	D5	Kolkata	45	D2	Chita	41	Q3
Bloemfontein	61	B3	Calgary	71	G4	Chittagong	45	E2
Blue Nile	55	G3	Cali	85	C2	Chongjin	51	B2
Bodo	21	C2	California	73		Chongqing	49	D4
Bogota	85	C2	California, Gulf of	79	A2	Christchurch	67	D6
Boise	77	B2	Callao	85	C4	Churchill	71	J4
Bolivia	85	D4	Camaguey	81	C2	Cincinnati	75	C3
Bologna	33	C2	Cambodia	47	B2	Ciudad Juarez	79	B1
Bolzano	33	C1	Cambrian			Clermont Ferrand	27	F4
Bombay =			Mountains	23	E4	Cleveland	75	C2
Mumbai	45	C3	Cambridge	23	G4	Cluj	35	C1
Bonifacio,			Cameroon	57	D2	Clutha, River	67	B7
Strait of	33	B4	Cameroon,			Coast Range	77	A3
Bonin Islands	62	H6	Mount	57	C2	Coats Land	89	A
Bonn	29	B3	Campbell Island	89	G	Cod, Cape	75	E2
Boothia, Gulf of	71	K3	Campeche,			Coimbatore	45	C3
Bordeaux	27	D4	Gulf of	79	C3	Coimbra	31	A3
Borneo	47	C3	Canada	71	J4	Cologne	29	B3
Bornholm	21	D4	Canary Islands	55	B2	Colombia	85	C2
Bosnia-			Canaveral, Cape	75	C4	Colombo	45	C4
Herzegovina	35	B2	Canberra	65	J7	Colorado	73	
Bosporus	35	D2	Cannes	27	H5	Colorado River	77	B3
Boston	75	D2	Cantabrian			Columbia, River	77	A2
Bothnia, Gulf of	21	E3	Mountains	31	B2	Columbus	75	C3
Botswana	61	B3	Canterbury	23	G5	Comorin, Cape	45	C4
Bouake	57	B2	Canterbury Bight	67	D7	Comoros	61	D2
Bougainville	62	J9	Canterbury Plains	67	D6	Conakry	57	A2
Boulogne	27	E1	Canton =			Concepcion	87	B3
Bourges	27	F3	Guangzhou	49	E4	Congo	59	A3

A			Alexander Island	89	L
Aachen	29	B3	Alexandria	55	G1
Aalborg	21	B4	Algarve	31	A5
Aarhus	21	C4	Algeria	55	D2
Aberdeen	23	E2	Algiers	55	D1
Aberystwyth	23	D4	Alicante	31	E4
Abidjan	57	B2	Alice Springs	65	F4
Abu Dhabi	43	E3	Alkmaar	25	C2
Abuja	57	C2	Alma Ata	41	M4
Acapulco	79	B3	Almeria	31	D5
Accra	57	B2	Alps	33	C1
Aconcagua	87	C3	Alsace	27	H2
Adamawa			Altai Mountains	49	C2
Highlands	57	D2	Amarillo	77	C3
Adana	43	C2	Amazon River	85	E3
Adare, Cape	89	G	American		
Addis Ababa	59	C2	Highland	89	D
Adelaide	65	G6	American		
Aden	43	D4	Samoa	63	N10
Aden, Gulf of	59	D1	Amersfoort	25	D2
Adriatic Sea	33	E3	Amiens	27	F2
Aegean Sea	35	C3	Amman	43	M9
Afghanistan	45	B1	Amritsar	45	C1
Africa	52–53		Amsterdam	25	C2
Agades	55	D3	Amundsen Sea	89	K
Agra	45	C2	Amur, River	41	S3
Ahmadabad	45	C2	Arnhem	25	D3
Ahvaz	43	D2	Arnhem Land	65	F2
Air	55	D3	Arnhem, Cape	65	G2
Aix	27	G5	Anadyr Range	41	W2
Ajaccio	33	B4	Anatolia	18	P7
Akita	51	E3	Anchorage	73	D2
Akureyri	21	J1	Ancona	33	D3
Al Aziziyah	55	E1	Andalusia	31	C5
Al Jawf	55	F2	Andaman Islands	47	A2
Alabama	73		Andes	82	C3
Aland Islands	21	E3	Andorra	31	F2
Alaska	73	D2	Angara, River	41	N3
Alaska Range	73	C2	Angers	27	D3
Alaska, Gulf of	73	D3	Anglesey	23	D4
Albacete	31	E4	Angola	61	A2
Albania	35	B2	Angouleme	27	E4
Albany (Australia)	65	C7	Anguilla	81	F3
Albany (USA)	75	C3	Ankara	43	C2
Albert, Lake	59	B2	Annapurna	45	D2
Alberta	71	G4	Annecy	27	H4
Alboran	31	D6	Annobon	57	C3
Albuquerque	77	C3	Anshan	49	F2
Aldemey	27	C2	Antananarivo	61	D2
Aleppo	43	C2	Antarctica	89	
Alesund	21	B3	Antarctic		
Aleutian Islands	62	L3	Peninsula	89	M
			Anticosti Island	71	M5
			Antigua &		
			Barbuda	81	F3

Antofagasta	87	B2	Avignon	27	G5
Antwerp	25	C3	Avon, River	23	F4
Aomori	51	E2	Axel Heiberg		
Aoraki Mount			Island	71	K2
Cook	67	B6	Ayers Rock	65	F5
Apeldoorn	25	D2	Azerbaijan	41	H4
Apennines	33	D3	Azores	55	A1
Appalachian			Azov, Sea of	37	G3
Mountains	75	C3			
Arabia	38	H6			
Arabian Sea	38	K7	**B**		
Arafura Sea	65	F1	Badajoz	31	B4
Aral Sea	41	K4	Baffin Bay	71	M2
Arctic Ocean	88		Baffin Island	71	L2
Ardennes	25	D5	Baghdad	43	D2
Arequipa	85	C4	Bahamas	81	C1
Argentina	87	C3	Bahia Blanca	87	C3
Arizona	73		Bahrain	43	E3
Arkansas	73		Baikal, Lake	41	P3
Arkansas River	75	B3	Baku	41	J4
Arkhangelsk	41	H2	Balearic Islands	31	F4
Armagh	23	C3	Bali	47	C4
Armenia	41	H5	Balikpapan	47	C4
Arnhem	25	D3	Balkan Mountains	35	C2
Arnhem Land	65	F2	Balkhash, Lake	41	L4
Arnhem, Cape	65	G2	Balleny Islands	89	G
Arran, Island	23	D3	Baltic Sea	21	D4
Aruba	81	D4	Baltimore	75	D3
Asahigawa	51	E2	Bamako	55	C3
Ascension Island	9	M7	Banda Sea	47	D4
Ashkhabad	41	J5	Bandar Seri		
Asia	38–39		Begawan	47	C3
Asmara	59	C1	Bandung	47	B4
Asuncion	87	D2	Bangalore =		
Aswan	55	G2	Bengaluru	45	C3
Asyut	55	G1	Bangka	47	B4
Atacama Desert	87	B2	Bangkok	47	B2
Athabasca,			Bangladesh	45	E2
Lake	71	H4	Bangui	59	A2
Athens	35	C3	Banjarmasin	47	C4
Athlone	23	C4	Banjul	57	A1
Atlanta	75	C3	Banks Island	71	F2
Atlantic Ocean	18	B3	Banks Peninsula	67	D6
Atlas Mountains	55	C1	Baotou	49	E2
Auckland	67	E3	Barbados	81	G4
Auckland Islands	89	G	Barcelona	31	G3
Augsburg	29	D4	Barcoo, River	65	H4
Austin	75	B3	Barents Sea	41	G1
Australia	64–65		Bari	33	F4
Australian Alps	65	J7	Barkly Tableland	65	G3
Austria	29	E5	Barranquilla	85	C1
Auvergne	27	F4			

Congo, Democratic
  Republic of the 59 B3
Congo, River 59 B2
Connecticut 73
Constance, Lake 29 C5
Constanta 35 D2
Constantine 55 D1
Cook Islands 63N10
Cook Strait 67 E5
Cook, Mount =
  Aoraki Mount
  Cook 67 B6
Copenhagen 21 C4
Coral Sea 65 J3
Cordoba
  (Argentina) 87 C3
Cordoba (Spain) 31 C5
Corfu 35 B3
Cork 23 B5
Coromandel
  Peninsula 67 E3
Corsica 33 B3
Cosenza 33 F5
Costa Blanca 31 E4
Costa Brava 31 G3
Costa del Sol 31 C5
Costa Rica 79 D4
Cote d'Ivoire 57 B2
Cotswolds 23 F5
Coventry 23 F4
Craiova 35 C2
Crete 35 D4
Crimea 37 F3
Croatia 35 B1
Crozet Islands 9 R10
Cuando, River 61 B2
Cuba 81 C2
Cubango, River 61 A2
Curaçao 81 E4
Curitiba 85 F5
Cuzco 85 C4
Cyprus 43 J5
Czechia 37 B3

D

Da Nang 47 B2
Daegu 51 B3
Daejeon 51 B3
Dakar 57 A1
Dakhla 55 B2
Dalian 49 F3
Dallas 75 B3
Damascus 43 C2
Dampier 65 C4
Danube, River 35 D2
Dar es Salaam 59 C3
Dardanelles 35 D3
Dargaville 67 D2
Darling Range 65 C6
Darling, River 65 H6
Darwin 65 E2
Davao 47 D3
Davis Strait 71 N3
Dawson 71 E3
Dead Sea 43 M9
Death Valley 77 B3
Deccan 45 C3
Delaware 73
Delhi 45 C2
Den Helder 25 C2
Denali 73 C2
Denmark 21 B4
Denver 77 C3
Derby 23 F4
Detroit 75 C2
Devon Island 71 K2
Dhaka 45 E2
Dieppe 27 E2
Dijon 27 G3
Dili 47 D4
Dinaric Alps 35 B2
District of
  Columbia 73
Djerid, Lake 55 D1
Djibouti 59 D1
Dnepr, River 37 F3
Dnepropetrovsk 37 F3
Dnestr, River 37 E3
Dodecanese 35 D3
Dodoma 59 C3
Dominica 81 F3
Dominican
  Republic 81 E3
Dondra Head 45 C4
Donetsk 37 G3
Dordogne, River 27 E4
Dordrecht 25 C3
Dortmund 29 B3
Douai 27 F1
Douala 57 D2
Douglas 23 D3
Douro, River 31 B3
Dover 23 G5
Dover, Strait of 23 G5
Drake's Passage 89 L
Drakensberg,
  Mountains 61 B3
Drava, River 35 B1
Dresden 29 E3
Duarte, Pico 81 D3
Dublin 23 C4
Dubrovnik 35 B2
Duero, River 31 D3
Duisburg 29 B3
Duluth 75 B2
Dundee 23 E2
Dunedin 67 C7
Dunkirk 27 F1
Durban 61 C3
Dushanbe 41 K5
Dusseldorf 29 B3
Dzungarian
  Desert =
  Junggar Pendi 49 B2

E

East China Sea 49 F4
East London 61 B4
Easter Islands 63 U11
Eastern Ghats 45 C3
Ebro, River 31 E3
Echo Bay 71 G3
Ecuador 85 C3
Edam 25 D2
Edinburgh 23 E3
Edmonton 71 G4
Edward, Lake 59 B3
Egadi Islands 33 D6
Egmont, Cape 67 D4
Egypt 55 F2
Eilat 43 C3
Eindhoven 25 D3
El Aaiun 55 B2
El Fasher 55 F3
El Obeid 55 G3
El Paso 77 C3
El Salvador 79 D3
Elba 33 C3
Elbe, River 29 C2
Elbrus, Mount 41 H4
Elburz Mountains 43 E2
Eleuthera Island 81 C1
Ellesmere Land 71 L2
Ellsworth Land 89 L
Ems, River 29 B2
Enderby Land 89 C
England 23 F4
English Channel 27 D1
Enschede 25 E2
Equatorial
  Guinea 57 C2
Erfurt 29 D3
Erie, Lake 75 C2
Eritrea 59 C1
Esbjerg 21 B4
Esfahan 43 E2
Espoo 21 E3
Essen 29 B3
Estonia 37 E1
Eswatini 61 C3
Ethiopia 59 D2
Ethiopian
  Highlands 59 C2
Etna, Mount 33 E6
Etosha Pan 61 A2
Eugene 77 A2
Euphrates, River 43 D2
Europe 18–19

Europoort 25 B2
Everest, Mount 49 B4
Everglades 75 C4
Evora 31 B4
Evre, Lake 65 G5

F

F'Derik 55 B2
Fairbanks 73 D2
Falkland Islands 87 C5
Farewell, Cape 67 D5
Fargo 75 B2
Faroe Islands 18 F2
Faya-Largeau 55 E3
Feza 55 C1
Fez 55 C1
Fiji 62 L6
Finisterre, Cape 31 A2
Finland 21 F3
Finland, Gulf of 21 F4
Firth of Forth 23 E2
Fitzroy, River 65 D3
Flanders 25 B3
Flensburg 29 C1
Flinders Ranges 65 G6
Florence 33 C3
Flores Sea 47 D4
Florida 73
Foggia 33 E4
Fort McMurray 71 G4
Fort Worth 75 B3
Fortaleza 85 G3
Fouta Djalon 57 A1
Foveaux Strait 67 B8
Foxe Channel 71 L3
France 27 E3
Frankfurt 29 C3
Franz Josef Land 41 N1
Fraser River 71 F4
Freeport 81 C1
Freetown 57 A2
Freiburg 29 B5
French Guiana 85 E2
French Polynesia 63Q10
Fresno 77 A3
Frisian Islands 25 C1
Fuji, Mount 51 D3
Fukuoka 51 C4
Fukushima 51 E3
Fushun 49 F2
Fuzhou 49 E4

G

Gabon 57 D3
Gaborone 61 B3
Gairdner, Lake 65 G6
Galapagos Islands 85 B3
Galati 35 D1
Galdhopiggen 21 B3
Galilee, Sea of 43 M8
Galway 23 B4
Gambia 57 A1
Ganges, River 45 D2
Gangneung 51 B3
Garda, Lake 33 C2
Garmo Peak 41 K4
Garonne, River 27 D4
Gascony 27 D5
Gävle 21 D3
Gaza Strip 43 L9
Gdansk 37 C2
Geelong 65 H7
Geneva 33 A1
Geneva, Lake 33 A1
Genoa 33 B2
George Town 47 B3
Georgetown 85 E2
Georgia 37 H4
Georgia (USA) 73
Gera 29 E3
Geraldton 65 B5
Germany 29 C3
Ghana 57 B2
Ghent 25 B3
Ghudamis 55 D1
Gibraltar 31 C5
Gibson Desert 65 D4

Gifu 51 D3
Gijon 31 C2
Gisborne 67 F4
Giza 55 G2
Glama, River 21 C3
Glasgow 23 D3
Gloucester 23 E5
Gobi Desert 49 D2
Godavari, River 45 C3
Godhavn 88 J
Godthaab =
  Nuuk 88 J
Goiania 85 E4
Good Hope,
  Cape of 61 A4
Gothenburg 21 C4
Gotland 21 D4
Gottingen 29 C3
Gouda 25 C2
Gozo 33 E6
Grampians 23 E2
Gran Chaco 87 C2
Granada 31 D5
Grand Bahama 81 C1
Grand Canyon 77 B3
Grand Cayman 81 B3
Graz 29 F5
Great Australia
  Bight 65 E6
Great Barrier
  Island 67 E3
Great Barrier
  Reef 65 J3
Great Basin 77 B3
Great Bear Lake 71 F3
Great Britain 18 G4
Great Divide 65 K6
Great Khingan
  Mountains 49 E2
Great Lakes 69 L4
Great Plains 77 D2
Great Salt Lake 77 B2
Great Sandy
  Desert 65 D4
Great Slave Lake 71 G3
Great Victoria
  Desert 65 E5
Great Wall of
  China 49 D3
Greater Antilles 81 C3
Greece 35 C3
Greenland 88 J
Greenland Sea 88 G
Grenada 81 F4
Grenoble 27 H4
Greymouth 67 C6
Groningen 25 E1
Grossglockner 29 E5
Guadalajara 79 B2
Guadalquivir,
  River 31 C5
Guadarrama,
  Sierra de 31 D3
Guadeloupe 81 F3
Guadiana, River 31 B5
Guam 62 H7
Guangzhou 49 E4
Guardafui, Cape 59 E1
Guatemala 79 C3
Guatemala City 79 C3
Guayaquil 85 B3
Guernsey 27 C2
Guilin 49 E4
Guinea 57 A1
Guinea, Gulf of 57 B2
Guinea-Bissau 57 A1
Guiyang 49 D4
Gunsan 51 B3
Guyana 85 E2
Gwangju 51 B3

H

Haarlem 25 C2
Hague, The 25 C2
Haida Gwaii 71 E4
Haifa 43 L8
Hainan 49 E5
Haiphong 47 B1
Haiti 81 D3

Hakodate 51 E2
Halifax 71 M5
Halle 29 E3
Halmahera 47 D3
Hamamatsu 51 D4
Hamburg 29 C2
Hamersley Range 65 C4
Hamhung 51 B3
Hamilton
  (Canada) 71 L5
Hamilton (NZ) 67 E3
Hanoi 47 B1
Hanover 29 C2
Harare 61 C2
Harbin 49 F2
Hardanger Fjord 21 B3
Harz Mountains 29 D3
Hastings 67 F4
Havana 81 B2
Hawaii 72 G2
Hawaiian Islands 72 F1
Hebrides 23 C2
Heidelberg 29 C4
Helsingborg 21 C4
Helsinki 21 F3
Herat 45 B1
Himalayas 45 D2
Hindu Kush 45 C1
Hiroshima 51 C4
Hispaniola 81 D3
Hitachi 51 E3
Ho Chi Minh City 47 B2
Hobart 65 J8
Hoggar 55 D2
Hokkaido 51 E2
Holyhead 23 D4
Honduras 79 D3
Hong Kong 49 E4
Honolulu 72 F1
Honshu 51 D3
Hook of Holland 25 C2
Horn, Cape 87 C5
Houston 75 B4
Huambo 61 A2
Huang He, River 49 E3
Huascaran 85 C3
Hudson Bay 71 K4
Hudson River 75 D2
Hudson Strait 71 L3
Huelva 31 B5
Hull 23 F4
Hungary 37 C3
Huron, Lake 75 C2
Hwang Ho =
  Huang He,
  River 49 E3
Hyderabad (India) 45 C3
Hyderabad
  (Pakistan) 45 B2
Hyesan 51 B2

I

Iasi 35 D1
Ibadan 57 C2
Iberian Peninsula 18 G6
Ibiza 31 F4
Iceland 21 J2
Idaho 73
IJssel, Lake 25 D2
Illinois 73
Iloilo 47 D2
Inari, Lake 21 F2
Incheon 51 B3
India 45 C2
Indian Ocean 38 L9
Indiana 73
Indianapolis 75 C2
Indonesia 47 C4
Indore 45 C2
Indus, River 45 B2
Inland Sea 51 C4
Inn, River 29 E4
Innsbruck 29 D5
Interlaken 33 B1
International
  Date Line 62 L5
Invercargill 67 B8
Inverness 23 E2
Katmandu 45 D2
Ionian Islands 35 B3

Ionian Sea 35 B3
Iowa 73
Ipswich 23 G4
Iquitos 85 C3
Iraklion 35 D3
Iran 43 E2
Iraq 43 D2
Irbid 43 M8
Ireland 23 C4
Irish Sea 23 D4
Irkutsk 41 P3
Iron Gates 35 C2
Irrawaddy, River 47 A1
Irtysh, River 41 L3
Islamabad 45 C1
Islay 23 C3
Israel 43 M8
Istanbul 43 B1
Italy 33 C3
Izmir 43 B2

J

Jabalpur 45 D2
Jacksonville 75 C3
Jaipur 45 C2
Jakarta 47 B4
Jamaica 81 C3
James Bay 71 K4
Japan 51 D3
Japan, Sea of 51 C3
Java 47 B4
Jedda 43 C3
Jeju-do 51 B4
Jerez 31 B5
Jersey 27 C2
Jerusalem 43 M9
Jinan 49 E3
Johannesburg 61 B3
Jonkoping 21 C4
Jordan 43 C2
Jordan, River 43 M8
Jotunheimen 21 B3
Juan Fernandez
  Island 63W12
Juba 55 G4
Jucar, River 31 E4
Juneau 71 E4
Junggar Pendi 49 B2
Jura 27 G3
Jutland 21 B4

K

K2 45 C1
Kabul 45 B1
Kaesong 51 B3
Kagoshima 51 C4
Kaikoura Range 67 D6
Kaimanawa
  Mountains 67 E4
Kalahari Desert 61 B3
Kalemie 59 B3
Kalgoorlie-Boulder 65 D6
Kamchatka
  Peninsula 41 U3
Kampala 59 C2
Kananga 59 B3
Kanazawa 51 D3
Kandahar 45 B1
Kangaroo Island 65 G7
Kanggye 51 B2
Kano 57 C1
Kanpur 45 D2
Kansas 73
Kansas City 75 B3
Kaohsiung 49 F4
Karachi 45 B2
Karaganda 41 L4
Karakoram
  Range 45 C1
Kariba, Lake 61 B2
Karlsruhe 29 C4
Kasai, River 59 B3
Kashmir 45 C1
Kassel 29 C3
Kati Thanda 65 G5
Katmandu 45 D2
Kattegat 21 C4

Kauai 72 E1
Kaunas 37 D1
Kawasaki 51 D3
Kazakhstan 41 K4
Kazan 41 H3
Keflavik 21 H2
Kemi 21 E2
Kemi, River 21 F2
Kentucky 73
Kenya 59 C2
Kerguelen 9 S10
Kermadec Islands 62 L11
Key West 75 C4
Khabarovsk 41 S4
Kharkov 37 G3
Khartoum 55 G3
Kiel 29 D1
Kiev 37 F2
Kigali 59 C3
Kikwit 59 A3
Kilimanjaro 59 C3
Kimberley
  (South Africa) 61 B3
Kimberley Plateau
  (Australia) 65 E3
Kimchaek 51 B2
Kinabalu 47 C3
Kingston 81 C3
Kinshasa 59 A3
Kinbati 62 L9
Kiritimati Island 63 P8
Kirkenes 21 F2
Kirov 41 H3
Kiruna 21 E2
Kisangani 59 B2
Kishinev 37 E3
Kismayu 59 D3
Kiso, River 51 D3
Kisumu 59 C3
Kitakami, River 51 E3
Kitakyushu 51 B4
Kitwe 61 B2
Klagenfurt 29 F5
Kobe 51 D4
Koblenz 29 B3
Kola Peninsula 41 G2
Kolkata =
  Calcutta 45 D2
Kolyma Range 41 U2
Korea Strait 51 B4
Kosciuszko,
  Mount 65 J7
Kosovo 35 C2
Krakatoa 47 B4
Krakow 37 C2
Krasnoyarsk 41 N3
Krishna, River 45 C3
Kristiansand 21 B4
Kuala Lumpur 47 B3
Kucing 47 C3
Kumamoto 51 C4
Kumasi 57 B2
Kunashir 51 F2
Kunlun Shan
  Mountains 49 B3
Kunming 49 D4
Kuopio 21 F3
Kuria Muria
  Islands 43 E4
Kuril Islands 62 J4
Kushiro 51 E2
Kuwait 43 D3
Kyoga, Lake 59 C2
Kyoto 51 D3
Kyrgyzstan 41 L4
Kyushu 51 C4

L

La Coruna 31 A2
La Paz 85 D4
La Plata 87 D3
La Rochelle 27 D3
La Spezia 33 B2
Labrador 71 M4
Laccadive
  Islands 45 C3
Lachlan, River 65 J6
Lagos (Nigeria) 57 C2
Lagos (Portugal) 31 A5

INDEX

Lahore 45 C1
Land's End 23 D5
Languedoc 27 F5
Lanzhou 49 D3
Laos 47 B2
Lapland 21 E2
Las Palmas 55 B2
Las Vegas 77 B3
Latvia 37 D1
Launceston 65 J8
Lausanne 33 A1
Le Havre 27 E2
Le Mans 27 D2
Lebanon 43 C2
Leeds 23 F4
Leeuwarden 25 D1
Leeuwin, Cape 65 B6
Leiden 25 C2
Leipzig 29 E3
Lek, River 25 C3
Lena, River 41 R2
Lens 27 F1
Leon (Mexico) 79 B2
Leon (Spain) 31 C2
Lerida 31 F3
Lesotho 61 B3
Lesser Antilles 81 F4
Lewis, Island 23 C1
Lhasa 49 C4
Liberia 57 B2
Libreville 57 D2
Libya 55 E2
Libyan Desert 55 F2
Liechtenstein 29 C5
Liege 25 D4
Ligurian Sea 33 B3
Likasi 59 B4
Lille 27 F1
Lillehammer 21 C3
Lilongwe 61 C2
Lima 85 C4
Limassol 43 J6
Limerick 23 B4
Limoges 27 E4
Limpopo, River 61 B3
Linares 31 D4
Line Islands 63 P9
Linkoping 21 D4
Linz 29 F4
Lions, Gulf of 27 G5
Lipari Islands 33 E5
Lisbon 31 A4
Lithuania 37 D1
Liverpool 23 E4
Livingstone 61 B2
Ljubljana 35 A1
Llanos 82 C2
Lobito 61 A2
Lodz 37 C2
Lofoten Islands 21 C2
Logan, Mount 71 E3
Loire, River 27 E3
Lome 57 C2
London (Canada) 71 K5
London (UK) 23 G5
Londonderry 23 C3
Lorient 27 C3
Lorraine 27 H2
Los Angeles 77 B3
Louisiana 73
Louisville 75 C3
Lourdes 27 E5
Lower California 79 A2
Lower Hutt 67 E5
Lualaba, River 59 B3
Luanda 61 A1
Lubango 61 A2
Lubeck 29 D2
Lubumbashi 59 B4
Lucknow 45 D2
Lugano 33 B1
Lule, River 21 E2
Lulea 21 E2
Lusaka 61 B2
Luton 23 F5
Luxembourg 25 E5
Luzern 33 B1
Luzon 47 D2
Lvov 37 D3
Lyons 27 G4

M
Maas, River 25 E3
Maastricht 25 D4
Macao 49 E4
Macdonnell Ranges 65 F4
Macedonia 35 C2
Machu Picchu 85 C4
Mackenzie River 71 F3
Macquarie Island 89 G
Madagascar 61 D3
Madeira 55 B1
Madeira, River 85 D3
Madrid 31 D3
Madras = Chennai 45 D3
Madurai 45 C4
Magadan 41 U3
Magdalena, River 85 C2
Magdeburg 29 D3
Magellan's Strait 87 B5
Mahajanga 61 D2
Maiduguri 57 D1
Main, River 29 D3
Maine 73
Majorca 31 G4
Makasar 47 C4
Makasar Strait 47 C4
Makgadikgadi Salt Pan 61 B3
Malabo 57 C2
Malacca, Straits of 47 B3
Malaga 31 C5
Malawi 61 C2
Malawi, Lake 61 C2
Malay Peninsula 38 P8
Malaysia 47 B3
Maldives 45 C4
Mali 55 C3
Malmo 21 C4
Malta 33 E6
Man, Isle of 23 D3
Manado 47 D3
Managua 79 D3
Manapouri, Lake 67 B7
Manaus 85 D3
Manchester 23 E4
Manchuria 49 F2
Mandalay 47 A1
Manila 47 C2
Manitoba 71 J4
Mannar, Gulf of 45 C4
Mannheim 29 C4
Maputo 61 C3
Maracaibo 85 C1
Margarita 81 F4
Maria van Diemen, Cape 67 C2
Mariana Trench 62 H7
Marie Byrd Land 89 J
Markham, Mount 89 G
Marquesas Islands 63 R9
Marrakesh 55 C1
Marseilles 27 G5
Marshall Islands 62 L7
Martinique 81 F4
Maryland 73
Maseru 61 B3
Mashhad 43 E2
Massachusetts 73
Massif Central 27 F4
Matadi 59 A3
Mato Grosso Plateau 85 E4
Matsuyama 51 C4
Maui 72 G1
Mauna Kea 72 G2
Mauna Loa 72 G2
Mauritania 55 B3
Mauritius 53 J7
Mayotte 61 D2
Mbabane 61 C3
Mbandaka 59 A2
Mbeya 59 C3
McKinley, Mount = Denali 73 C2
Mecca 43 C3
Medan 47 A3

Medellin 85 C2
Medicine Hat 71 G5
Medina 43 C3
Mediterranean Sea 19 K7
Mekong, River 47 B2
Melanesia 62 J9
Melbourne 65 J7
Melilla 31 D6
Melville Island (Canada) 71 G2
Melville Islands (Australia) 65 F2
Memphis 75 C3
Mendoza 87 C3
Mentawai Islands 47 A4
Meseta 31 C4
Mesopotamia 43 D2
Messina (Italy) 33 E5
Messina (South Africa) 61 B3
Metz 27 H2
Meuse, River 25 D4
Mexico 79 B2
Mexico City 79 B2
Mexico, Gulf of 79 D2
Miami 75 D4
Michigan 73
Michigan, Lake 75 C2
Micronesia 62 K8
Middlesbrough 23 F3
Midway Island 62 M6
Mikonos 35 D3
Milan 33 B2
Milwaukee 75 B2
Mindanao 47 D3
Minho, River 31 A2
Minneapolis 75 B2
Minnesota 73
Minorca 31 G4
Minsk 37 E2
Mississippi River 75 B3
Mississippi, State 73
Missouri, State 73
Mitchell, Mount 75 C3
Mjosa, Lake 21 C3
Mogadishu 59 D2
Moldova 37 E3
Molokai 72 F1
Molucca Sea 47 D4
Mombasa 59 D3
Monaco 27 H5
Mongolia 49 D2
Mongu 61 B2
Monrovia 57 A2
Mons 25 B4
Montana 73
Montbeliard 27 H3
Montego Bay 81 C3
Montenegro 35 B2
Monterrey 79 B2
Montevideo 87 D3
Montgomery 75 C3
Montpellier 27 F5
Montreal 71 L5
Montserrat 81 F3
Moorea 63 Q10
Morava, River 35 C2
Morena, Sierra 31 C4
Morocco 55 C1
Moscow 41 G3
Moselle, River 27 H2
Moshi 59 C3
Mosul 43 D2
Moulmein 47 A2
Mount Isa 65 G4
Mozambique 61 C2
Mozambique Channel 61 D2
Mulhacen 31 D5
Mulhouse 27 H3
Mull, Island 23 C2
Multan 45 C1
Mumbai 45 C2
Munich 29 D4
Munster 29 B3
Muonio, River 21 E2
Mur, River 29 F5
Murcia 31 E5
Murray, River 65 H6

Murrumbidgee, River 65 J6
Musala 35 C2
Muscat 43 E3
Musgrave Ranges 65 F5
Mutare 61 C2
Mwanza 59 C3
Mweru, Lake 59 B3
Myanmar 47 A1

N
Nafud Desert 43 D3
Nagasaki 51 B4
Nagoya 51 D3
Nagpur 45 D2
Nairobi 59 C3
Namib Desert 61 A3
Namibia 61 A3
Namur 25 C4
Nan Shan Mountains 49 C3
Nanchang 49 E4
Nancy 27 H2
Nanjing 49 E3
Nantes 27 D3
Nao, Cabo de la 31 F4
Napier 67 F4
Naples 33 E4
Nara 51 D4
Narmada, River 45 C2
Narvik 21 D2
Nashville 75 C3
Nassau 81 C1
Nasser, Lake 55 G2
Nauru 62 K9
Naypyidaw 47 A2
Nazare 31 A4
Nazareth 43 M8
Ndjamena 55 E3
Ndola 61 B2
Neagh, Lough 23 C3
Nebraska 73
Negro, River 85 D3
Neisse, River 29 F3
Nelson 67 D5
Nelson, River 71 J4
Nemuro Strait 51 F2
Nepal 45 D2
Netherlands 25 E2
Nevada 73
Nevada, Sierra 31 C5
New Brunswick 71 M5
New Caledonia 62 K11
New Castile 31 C4
New Guinea 62 H9
New Hampshire 73
New Jersey 73
New Mexico 73
New Orleans 75 C4
New Plymouth 67 D4
New Siberian Islands 41 U1
New South Wales 65 J6
New York 75 D2
New York State 73
New Zealand 66–67
Newcastle (Australia) 65 K6
Newcastle-upon-Tyne (UK) 23 F3
Newfoundland 71 N5
Newman 65 C4
Niagara Falls 71 L5
Niamey 55 D3
Nicaragua 79 D3
Nice 27 H5
Nicobar Islands 47 A3
Nicosia 43 J5
Niger 55 D3
Niger, River 57 C1
Nigeria 57 C2
Niigata 51 D3
Nijmegen 25 D3
Nile, River 55 G2
Nimes 27 G5
Nis 35 C2
Nizhniy Novgorod 41 H3

Nome 73 B2
Norfolk 75 D3
Normandy 27 E2
Norrkoping 21 D4
North America 68–69
North Cape 21 E1
North Carolina 73
North Dakota 73
North European Plain 18 L4
North Island, New Zealand 67 E4
North Korea 51 B3
North Magnetic Pole 88 M
North Pole 88
North Sea 18 H3
North West Highlands 23 D2
Northampton 23 F4
Northern Ireland 23 C3
Northwest Territories 71 H3
Northern Territory 65 F3
Norway 21 C3
Norwich 23 G4
Nottingham 23 F4
Nouakchott 55 B3
Nova Scotia 71 M5
Novaya Zemlya 41 J1
Novosibirsk 41 M3
Nullarbor Plain 65 E6
Nunavut 71 K3
Nuremberg 29 D4
Nuuk 88 J

O
Oahu 72 E1
Oamaru 67 C7
Ob, River 41 K2
Oban 23 D2
Odense 21 C4
Oder, River 29 F2
Odessa 37 F3
Ogbomosho 57 C2
Ogooue, River 57 D3
Ohio 73
Ohio River 75 C3
Okavango Swamp 61 B2
Okayama 51 C4
Okhotsk, Sea of 41 T3
Oki Islands 51 C3
Oklahoma 73
Oklahoma City 77 D3
Oland 21 D4
Old Castile 31 C3
Oldenburg 29 C2
Omaha 75 B2
Oman 43 E3
Oman, Gulf of 43 E3
Omdurman 55 G3
Omsk 41 L3
Ontario 71 K4
Ontario, Lake 75 D2
Oporto 31 A3
Oran 55 C1
Orange 27 G4
Orange, River 61 A3
Ore Mountains 29 E3
Orebro 21 C4
Oregon 73
Orense 31 B2
Orinoco, River 85 D2
Orizaba, Pico de 79 C3
Orkney Islands 23 E1
Orleans 27 E3
Osaka 51 D4
Oslo 21 C4
Ostend 25 A3
Ostersund 21 D3
Otaru 51 E2
Otranto, Strait of 33 G4
Ottawa 71 L5
Ouagadougou 57 B1
Oulu 21 F3
Oulu, Lake 21 F3
Oviedo 31 C2

Oxford 23 F5

P
Pacific Ocean 62 K6
Padang 47 B4
Padua 33 C2
Pakistan 45 B2
Palau 62 G8
Palawan 47 C2
Palembang 47 B4
Palermo 33 D5
Palm Beach 75 D4
Palma 31 G4
Palmerston North 67 E5
Pampas 87 C3
Pamplona 31 E2
Panama 79 E4
Panama Canal 79 D3
Pantellaria 33 D6
Papua New Guinea 62 H9
Paraguay 87 D2
Paramaribo 85 E2
Parana River 87 D2
Paris 27 F2
Parma 33 C2
Patagonia 87 C4
Patrai 35 C3
Pau 27 D5
Peace River 71 G4
Pegasus Bay 67 D6
Peking = Beijing 49 E2
Pemba 59 C3
Pennines 23 E3
Pennsylvania 73
Penzance 23 D5
Perm 41 J3
Perpignan 27 F6
Persian Gulf, The 43 E3
Perth (Australia) 65 C6
Perth (UK) 23 E2
Peru 85 C4
Perugia 33 D3
Pescara 33 E3
Philadelphia 75 D3
Philippines 47 C2
Phnom Penh 47 B2
Phoenix 77 B3
Phoenix Islands 62 M9
Picardy 27 F2
Pietermaritzberg 61 C3
Pilatus, Mount 33 B1
Pindus Mountains 35 C3
Pisa 33 C3
Pitcairn Island 63 S11
Pittsburgh 75 C2
Plata, Rio de la 87 D3
Plenty, Bay of 67 F3
Ploiesti 35 D2
Plovdiv 35 D2
Plymouth 23 D5
Po, River 33 C2
Podgorica 35 B2
Pohang 51 B3
Pointe-Noire 59 A3
Poitiers 27 E3
Poland 37 C2
Polar Plateau 89 C
Polynesia 63 N8
Pontianak 47 B4
Poopo, Lake 85 D4
Port Elizabeth 61 B4
Port Harcourt 57 C2
Port of Spain 81 F4
Port Pirie 65 G6
Port Said 55 G1
Port Sudan 55 G3
Port Talbot 23 E5
Port-au-Prince 81 D3
Portland 77 A2
Porto Alegre 85 F5
Porto-Novo 57 C2
Portsmouth 23 F5
Portugal 31 B4
Potsdam 29 E2
Prague 37 B2
Prairies 70
Pretoria 61 B3
Prince Edward Island 71 M5
Prince George 71 F4
Prince Rupert 71 F4

Pripet, River 37 E2
Pristina 35 C2
Provence 27 G5
Providence 75 D3
Prudhoe Bay 73 C2
Prut, River 35 D1
Prydz Bay 89 D
Puebla 79 C3
Pueblo 77 C3
Puerto Rico 81 E3
Pune 45 C3
Punta Arenas 87 B5
Pyongyang 51 B3
Pyrenees 31 F2

Q
Qatar 43 E3
Qingdao 49 F3
Qiqihar 49 F2
Quebec 71 L5
Queen Elizabeth Islands 71 J2
Queen Maud Land 89 B
Queensland 65 H4
Queenstown 67 B7
Quetta 45 B1
Quezon City 47 D2
Quimper 27 B2
Quito 85 C3

R
Rabat 55 C1
Race, Cape 71 N5
Ravenna 33 D2
Rawalpindi 45 C1
Reading 23 F5
Recife 85 G3
Red Sea 43 C3
Red, River (USA) 75 B3
Red, River (Vietnam) 47 B1
Regensburg 29 E4
Reggio 33 E5
Regina 71 H4
Reims 27 G2
Reindeer Lake 71 H4
Rennes 27 D2
Reno 77 B3
Réunion 53 J8
Revilla Gigedo Islands 79 A3
Reykjavik 21 H2
Rhine, River 29 B3
Rhode Island 73
Rhodes 35 D3
Rhodope 35 C2
Rhone, River 27 G4
Richmond 75 D3
Riga 37 D1
Rimini 33 D2
Rio de Janeiro 85 F5
Rio Grande, River 77 D4
Rio Muni 57 D2
Riviera 33 B2
Riyadh 43 D3
Rockhampton 65 K4
Rocky Mountains 68 H4
Romania 35 C1
Rome 33 D4
Ronne Ice Shelf 89 L
Rosa, Monte 33 B2
Rosario 87 C3
Ross Ice Shelf 89 H
Ross Sea 89 H
Rostock 29 E1
Rostov 41 G4
Rotorua 67 F4
Rotterdam 25 C3
Rouen 27 E2
Rub 'al Khali 43 D4
Rugen 29 F1
Ruhr, River 29 B3

Entry	Page	Grid
Ruse	35	D2
Russia	41	L2
Rwanda	59	C3
Ryukyu Islands	38	R6

S

Entry	Page	Grid
Saarbrucken	29	B4
Saaremaa	37	D1
Sabah	47	C3
Sable, Cape (Canada)	71	M5
Sable, Cape (USA)	75	C4
Sacramento	77	A3
Sado	51	D3
Sahara	55	D2
Sahel	52	C4
Saimaa, Lake	21	F3
Saint Etienne	27	G4
Saint Gallen	33	B1
Saint George's Channel	23	C5
Saint Gotthard tunnel	33	B1
Saint Helena	52	C7
Saint John	71	M5
Saint John's	71	N5
Saint Kitts & Nevis	81	F3
Saint Lawrence, River	71	M5
Saint Louis	75	B3
Saint Lucia	81	F4
Saint Malo	27	C2
Saint Nazaire	27	C3
Saint Paul	75	B2
Saint Petersburg	41	G3
Saint Pierre & Miquelon	71	N5
Saint Vincent & the Grenadines	81	F4
Sakai	51	D4
Sakhalin	41	T3
Salamanca	31	C3
Salerno	33	E4
Salt Lake City	77	B2
Salvador	85	G4
Salween, River	47	A2
Salzburg	29	E5
Samara	41	J3
Samoa	62	M10
San Antonio	75	B4
San Diego	77	B3
San Francisco	77	A3
San Jose (Costa Rica)	79	D3
San Jose (USA)	77	A3
San Juan	81	E3
San Lucas, Cape	79	A2
San Marino	33	C3
San Salvador	79	C3
San Sebastian	31	E2
San'a	43	D4
Santa Fe	87	D3
Santander	31	D2
Santarem	31	A4
Santiago (Chile)	87	B3
Santiago (Dominican Republic)	81	D3
Santiago de Cuba	81	D3
Santo Domingo	81	E3
Sao Francisco, River	85	F4
Sao Paulo	85	F5
São Tomé & Príncipe	57	C2
Saone, River	27	G3
Sapporo	51	E2
Sarajevo	35	B2
Sarawak	47	C3
Sardinia	33	B4
Sarh	55	E4
Saskatchewan	71	H4
Saskatoon	71	H4
Sassari	33	B4
Saudi Arabia	43	D3
Sault Sainte Marie	71	K5
Sayan Mountains	41	N3
Scandinavia	18	K2
Schelde, River	25	C3
Schwerin	29	D2
Scilly, Isles of	23	C6
Scotland	23	D2
Seattle	77	A2
Segura, River	31	E4
Seine, River	27	F2
Selvas	82	D3
Semarang	47	C4
Sendai	51	E3
Senegal	57	A1
Senegal, River	55	B3
Seoul	51	B3
Serbia	35	C2
Sevastopol	37	F4
Severn, River	23	E4
Severnaya Zemlya	88	D
Seville	31	B5
Sfax	55	E1
Shanghai	49	F3
Shannon, River	23	B4
Sheffield	23	F4
Shenyang	49	F2
Shetland Islands	23	G1
Shibeli, River	59	D2
Shikoku	51	C4
Shiraz	43	E3
Siberia	41	N2
Sicily	33	D6
Sidra, Gulf of	55	E1
Siena	33	C3
Sierra Leone	57	A2
Sierra Madre	79	B2
Sierra Nevada	77	B3
Sikhote Alin Range	41	S4
Sinai	52	G3
Singapore	47	B3
Sinuiju	51	A2
Sioux Falls	75	B2
Siracusa	33	E6
Sjaelland	21	C4
Skagerrak	21	B4
Skopje	35	C2
Skovorodino	41	R3
Skye, Island	23	C2
Slovak Republic	37	C3
Slovenia	35	A1
Snake River	77	B2
Snowdon	23	D4
Society Islands	63	P10
Socotra	43	E4
Sofia	35	C2
Sogne Fjord	21	B3
Solomon Islands	62	K9
Somali Republic	59	D2
Somerset Islands	71	J2
Songhua Jiang, River	49	G2
Sorano	33	C3
South Africa	61	B3
South America	82–83	
South Australia	65	G5
South Carolina	73	
South China Sea	47	C2
South Dakota	73	
South Georgia	89	M
South Island, New Zealand	67	C6
South Korea	51	B3
South Magnetic Pole	89	F
South Orkney Islands	89	M
South Pole	89	
South Sandwich Islands	89	A
South Shetland Islands	89	M
South Sudan	55	F4
Southampton	23	F5
Southampton Island	71	K3
Southern Alps	67	C6
Southern Ocean	65	D7
Southern Uplands	23	D3
Spain	31	C4
Spenser Mountains	67	D6
Spiez	33	A1
Split	35	B2
Spokane	77	B2
Sri Lanka	45	D4
Srinagar	45	C1
Stanley	87	D5
Stanovoy Range	41	R3
Stavanger	21	B4
Stewart Island	67	A8
Stockholm	21	D4
Stoke-on-Trent	23	E4
Storsjon	21	C3
Strasbourg	27	H2
Stuttgart	29	C4
Sucre	85	D4
Sudan	55	F3
Sudbury	71	K5
Suez	55	G2
Sulawesi	47	D4
Sulu Islands	47	D3
Sulu Sea	47	D3
Sumatra	47	B4
Sumbawa	47	C4
Sunda Islands	47	C4
Sunderland	23	F3
Sundsvall	21	D3
Superior, Lake	75	C2
Surabaya	47	C4
Surat	45	C2
Suriname	85	E2
Surtsey	21	H2
Svalbard	88	G
Sverdrup Islands	71	H2
Swansea	23	D5
Sweden	21	D3
Switzerland	33	B1
Sydney	65	K6
Syria	43	C2
Syrian Desert	43	C2

T

Entry	Page	Grid
Ta'izz	43	D4
Tabora	59	C3
Tabriz	43	D2
Tagus, River	31	A4
Tahiti	63	Q10
Tainaron, Cape	35	C3
Taipei	49	F4
Taiwan	49	F4
Taiyuan	49	E3
Tajikistan	41	L5
Takla Makan Mountains	49	B3
Tallinn	37	D1
Tampa	75	C4
Tampere	21	E3
Tana, Lake	59	C1
Tana, River (Kenya)	59	C2
Tana, River (Norway)	21	F2
Tanami Desert	65	F3
Tanega Island	51	C4
Tanga	59	C3
Tanganyika, Lake	59	C3
Tangier	55	C1
Tangshan	49	E3
Tanzania	59	C3
Tapajos, River	85	E3
Taranaki, Mount	67	E4
Taranto	33	F4
Tarim He, River	49	B2
Tarragona	31	F3
Tashkent	41	K4
Tasman Bay	67	D5
Tasmania	65	H8
Tatra Mountains	37	C3
Taupo, Lake	67	E4
Taurus Mountains	43	C2
Taymyr Peninsula	41	P1
Tbilisi	41	H4
Te Anau, Lake	67	B7
Tegucigalpa	79	D3
Tehran	43	E2
Tel Aviv-Jaffa	43	L8
Tema	57	C2
Tennessee	73	
Tennessee River	75	C3
Temi	33	D3
Texas	73	
Thabana Ntlenyana	61	C3
Thailand	47	B2
Thailand, Gulf of	47	B3
Thames, River	23	F5
Thessaloniki	35	C2
Thimphu	45	D2
Thionville	27	H2
Thule	88	K
Thunder Bay	71	K5
Tian Shan Mountains	49	B2
Tianjin	49	E3
Tiber, River	33	D3
Tibesti	55	E2
Tibet	49	B3
Tierra del Fuego	87	C5
Tigris, River	43	D2
Tijuana	79	A1
Tilburg	25	D3
Timaru	67	C7
Timbuktu	55	C3
Timisoara	35	C1
Timor-Leste	47	D4
Timor Sea	65	D2
Tirane	35	B2
Tirol	29	D6
Titicaca, Lake	85	D4
Togo	57	C2
Tokelau Islands	62	M9
Tokyo	51	D3
Toledo (Spain)	31	D4
Toledo (USA)	75	C2
Toliara	61	D3
Tone, River	51	D3
Tonga	62	M11
Toowoomba	65	K5
Torne, River	21	E2
Toronto	71	L5
Torrens, Lake	65	G6
Torreon	79	B2
Torres Strait	65	H1
Toubkal	55	C1
Toulon	27	G5
Toulouse	27	E5
Tours	27	E3
Townsville	65	J3
Toyama	51	D3
Transylvanian Alps	35	C1
Trent, River	23	F4
Trieste	33	D2
Trinidad & Tobago	81	G4
Tripoli	55	E1
Tromso	21	D2
Trondheim	21	C3
Troyes	27	G2
Trujillo	85	C3
Tsangpo, River	49	B4
Tsugaru, Strait	51	E2
Tsushima	51	B4
Tuamotu Archipelago	63	R10
Tubuai Islands	63	P11
Tucson	77	B3
Tucuman	87	C2
Tulsa	75	B3
Tunis	55	E1
Tunisia	55	D1
Turin	33	B2
Turkana, Lake	59	C2
Turkey	43	C2
Turkmenistan	41	J5
Turks Islands	81	D2
Turku	21	E3
Tuvalu	62	L9
Tyrrhenian Sea	33	D5

U

Entry	Page	Grid
Ubangi, River	59	A2
Udine	33	D1
Uganda	59	C2
Ukraine	37	F3
Ulan Bator	49	D2
Ulan Ude	41	P3
Ulsan	51	B3
Uluru = Ayers Rock	65	F5
Ume, River	21	D3
United Arab Emirates	43	E3
United Kingdom	23	G4
United States of America	72	
Uppsala	21	D4
Ural Mountains	41	J3
Ural, River	41	J4
Urmia, Lake	43	D2
Uruguay	87	D3
Ürümqi	49	B2
Ushant	27	B2
Utah	73	
Utrecht	25	D2
Uzbekistan	41	K4

V

Entry	Page	Grid
Vaal, River	61	B3
Vaasa	21	E3
Valence	27	G4
Valencia	31	E4
Valenciennes	27	F1
Valladolid	31	C3
Valletta	33	E6
Valparaiso	87	B3
Van, Lake	43	D2
Vancouver	71	F5
Vancouver Island	71	F5
Vaner, Lake	21	C4
Vantaa	21	E3
Vanuatu	62	K10
Varanasi	45	D2
Vardo	21	G1
Varna	35	D2
Vasteras	21	D4
Vatican City	33	C4
Vatnajokull	21	J2
Vatter, Lake	21	C4
Venezuela	85	D2
Venice	33	D2
Verkhoyansk Range	41	R2
Vermont	73	
Verona	33	C2
Versailles	27	F2
Vesteralen	21	C2
Vesuvius	33	E4
Victoria (Australia)	65	H7
Victoria (Canada)	71	F5
Victoria Falls	61	B2
Victoria Island	71	G2
Victoria Land	89	G
Victoria, Lake	59	C3
Vienna	29	F4
Vientiane	47	B2
Vietnam	47	B2
Vigo	31	A2
Vilnius	37	E2
Virgin Islands	81	F3
Virginia	73	
Viscount Melville Sound	71	H2
Vishakhapatnam	45	D3
Vistula, River	37	D2
Vitoria	31	D2
Vladivostok	41	S4
Volga, River	41	H3
Volgograd	41	H4
Volos	35	C3
Volta, Lake	57	B2
Vosges	27	H2

W

Entry	Page	Grid
Waal, River	25	D3
Wadden Zee	25	D1
Wadi Halfa	55	G2
Waikato, River	67	E4
Waitaki, River	67	C7
Wake Island	62	K7
Wakkanai	51	E1
Walcheren Island	25	B3
Wales	23	E4
Walvis Bay	61	A3
Wanaka, Lake	67	B7
Wanganui	67	E4
Warrego, River	65	J5
Warsaw	37	D2
Wasatch Range	77	B3
Wash, The	23	G4
Washington	75	D3
Washington, State	73	
Waterford	23	C4
Weddell Sea	89	M
Weipa	65	H2
Wellington	67	E5
Weser, River	29	C2
West Bank	43	M8
West Indies	80–81	
West Virginia	73	
Western Australia	65	D5
Western Ghats	45	C3
Western Sahara	55	B2
Westland Bight	67	B6
Wexford	23	C4
Whangarei	67	E2
White Nile	55	G4
White Sea	41	G2
Whitehorse	71	E3
Whitney, Mount	77	B3
Whyalla	65	G6
Wichita	75	B3
Wick	23	E1
Wicklow Mountains	23	C4
Wiesbaden	29	C3
Wight, Isle of	23	F5
Wilkes Land	89	F
Windhoek	61	A3
Windsor	71	K5
Windward Passage	81	D3
Winnipeg	71	J5
Winnipeg, Lake	71	J4
Winterthur	33	B1
Wisconsin	73	
Wollongong	65	K6
Wonsan	51	B3
Worcester	23	E4
Wrangel Island	41	W1
Wroclaw	37	C2
Wuhan	49	E3
Wurzburg	29	D4
Wye, River	23	E4
Wyndham	65	E3
Wyoming	73	

X

Entry	Page	Grid
Xi Jiang, River	49	D4
Xian	49	D3

Y

Entry	Page	Grid
Yakutsk	41	R2
Yamoussoukro	57	B2
Yangon	47	A2
Yangtze = Chang Jiang, River	49	E3
Yaounde	57	D2
Yekaterinburg	41	K3
Yellow Sea	49	F3
Yellowknife	71	G3
Yellowstone, River	77	C2
Yemen	43	D4
Yenisey, River	41	M2
Yerevan	41	H4
Yokohama	51	D3
York	23	F4
York, Cape	65	H2
Yucatan	79	D3
Yukon	71	E3
Yukon, River	73	C2

Z

Entry	Page	Grid
Zagreb	35	B1
Zagros Mountains	43	E2
Zambezi, River	61	C2
Zambia	61	B2
Zamboanga	47	D3
Zanzibar	59	C3
Zaragoza	31	E3
Zaria	57	C1
Zeebrugge	25	B3
Zhengzhou	49	E3
Zimbabwe	61	B2
Zurich	33	B1
Zwolle	25	E2

GLOSSARY

GLOSSARY

Arable farming – growing crops.

Border – the line along which two countries meet. Country borders are shown by red lines on all the maps in this atlas (see p. 16).

Canal – a man-made waterway that allows boats to travel from one ocean or place to another (examples on pp. 32, 34, 54, 79).

Canyon – a deep, steep-sided valley, usually cut by a river in a desert area. The most famous is the Grand Canyon (p. 76). A small canyon is called a gorge (examples on pp. 28, 34).

Capital city – the city where the government of a country meets. Every capital city is underlined on the maps in this atlas (explained on p. 16).

Continent – a very large land-mass. Of the 7 continents (pp. 2, 6-7) only Australia and Antarctica are not divided into countries.

Coral – tiny creatures which live in the sea. When they die, their shells join together to make coral reefs (p. 64) and islands (p. 62).

Core – the inner part of the Earth (p. 4).

Crops – plants grown for people or animals. There are many examples in this atlas: fruit and vegetables (pp. 34, 56, 66); rice (pp. 45, 46); wheat (p. 76); tea (pp. 44,50); oil-palm (p. 57).

Crust – the outer layer of the Earth (p. 4).

Delta – an area where mud and sand are dumped at the mouth of some rivers. Deltas occur where the river dumps more sand and mud than currents in the sea or lake can carry away. The River Nile has a large delta (p. 55) and so does the Mississippi (p.75). The name comes from the 4th letter of the Greek alphabet - find its shape on p. 35.

Desert – a large dry area where very little grows (pp. 14-15). The Sahara is the largest desert (pp. 11, 55); the Atacama is the driest (see the map on p.87).

Earthquake – a sudden movement in the Earth's crust causes shock waves which make the Earth's surface shake. Earthquakes are recorded on a seismograph.

Exports – the products of a country which are sold to other countries. They may be crops (p. 66); animals or meat; wood or minerals; or goods produced in factories or workshops.

Fjord – a long, steep-sided inlet of the sea. Once it was a valley eroded by a glacier, but after the glacier melted, the valley was drowned when the sea level rose. There are beautiful fjords in Norway (p. 20), New Zealand and Chile.

Geothermal power – electricity is made from steam which rises from the ground in some volcanic areas (p. 67).

Geyser – a hot spring which throws out a jet of hot water. Geysers are found in volcanic areas where the water is heated underground (pp. 67, 86).

Glacier – a mass of ice which flows downhill very slowly along a valley. As it moves, it makes the valley deeper and straighter. (p. 45 and the satellite image on p. 5).

Hurricane – a severe storm with very strong winds (up to 340 km per hour!) which cause a lot of damage (p. 81). Heavy rain and high tides may cause flooding, too. The same kind of storm is also called a cyclone or typhoon.

Hydro-electric power – electricity is made by water rushing through turbines in a power station. The water may come from a waterfall – as at the Niagara Falls (p. 70) – or from behind a man-made dam (p. 22).

Ice Age – a time in the Earth's history when the climate was much colder than today and ice spread over large areas of the world. Rocks we see today may have been shaped by ice during the last Ice Age (p. 23).

Iceberg – lump of floating ice, most of which is underwater. It may be small or really big (pp. 19, 88).

Ice-sheet – a huge, thick area of ice which is slowly moving outwards. The largest ice-sheet covers Antarctica (p. 89).

Irrigation – watering the land to help crops grow when the weather is dry. Often, people dig channels from a lake or river to the edge of fields. When they want to water the field, they make gaps to let the water flow over the land (p. 45).

Jungle, or rainforest – thick forest with large trees in hot, wet parts of the world near the Equator (see map p. 15 and pp. 13, 84).

Lake – an area of water that is surrounded by land. Find examples on pp. 5, 14, 20, 29, 40, 74, 75, 82.

Land-locked countries – countries that do not have any coastline or ports. This makes it more difficult and expensive to send exports or get imports from other countries (pp. 37, 60, 87).

Marshland – land that is wet and soggy because the water on it cannot drain away (pp. 22, 88).

Minerals – rocks which are mined or quarried and used in different kinds of industry. Iron ore, gold and bauxite (for aluminium) are examples.

Monsoon – explained on p. 45.

Oasis – an area in a desert with water at or near the surface. People can live there and use the water from springs or wells to grow crops or keep animals (p. 54).

Ocean – a huge area of sea-water covering a large part of the Earth's surface (p. 6-7). The largest is the Pacific (pp. 62-63).

Pasture – grass grown or used for feeding animals (pp. 19, 66, 85).

Peninsula – an area of land almost completely surrounded by water, but joined to the mainland at one point.

Plain – an area of low land with a fairly level surface, though there may be some low hills. It is (or was) often grassland (pp. 6, 18, 70).

Plantation – a very large farm where only one crop is grown. This is sold for export or to be used in factories. For example, tea (pp. 44, 50) and oil-palm (p. 56).

Plateau – an area of high land with a fairly level surface. Some plateaus are divided by deep valleys (pp. 30, 38, 49, 78).

Polar – to do with the area near the North or South Poles, inside the Arctic or Antarctic Circles (pp. 12, 88–89).

Population – the number of people in a country or city or area of the world (p. 20).

Port – a town or city at or near the sea or on a navigable river where ships can tie up to load or unload goods (pp. 24, 49, 70, 87).

Savanna – tropical grassland, often with some scattered trees. The weather is hot all year but there is a wet season when the tall grass is green and good for the animals to eat, and a dry season when the grass turns brown and dry (pp. 14-15, 58).

Season – a time of the year with distinct weather. People in temperate lands talk about hot and cold seasons (summer and winter). People in many tropical areas talk about wet and dry seasons. The reason for seasons is explained on p. 12.

Semi-desert – an area that is mainly dry, but small amounts of rain allow some plants to grow.

Temperate lands – parts of the world between the tropics and the polar areas which have a cold season (winter) and a hot season (summer) (see p. 12).

Terraces – wide steps cut into a hillside to make flat land for farming (p. 46). They also stop soil erosion.

Tropical areas – parts of the world between the Tropic of Cancer and the Tropic of Capricorn. Here the climate is hot, and the sun is overhead at midday twice each year (explained on pp. 12–13).

Tsunami – a huge wave caused by an earthquake under the bed of the sea (mentioned on pp. 4, 38, 50).

Tundra – an area around the Arctic Circle where it is too cold for trees to grow. Lichens and small plants grow, but deep down the soil is frozen even in summer (pp. 14, 20, 88).

Valley – a low area between mountains or hills which has been made by a river or glacier (pp. 22, 45).

Volcano – a mountain or hill made of lava and ash that has come from inside the Earth's crust. Active volcanoes are still sending out lava, ash and gases (pp. 5, 21, 33, 50, 72). Those that are no longer active are called 'dormant' (meaning 'sleeping') or extinct (p. 59).

Waterfall – the place where a river falls over a layer of hard rocks. Famous waterfalls are the Victoria Falls (p. 60) and the Niagara Falls (p. 70).

ANSWERS TO QUESTIONS

Page 4 Atlantic Ocean; Indian Ocean; South America; Brazil.

Page 6 Vicuña in the Andes of Argentina, South America.

Page 18 Brussels, Belgium: it is the headquarters of the European Union.

Page 22 The London landmarks featured on the stamp are *(from left to right)*: Westminster Abbey; Nelson's Column (in Trafalgar Square); statue of Eros (in Piccadilly Circus); Telecom Tower; clock tower of the Houses of Parliament (containing the bell Big Ben); St Paul's Cathedral; Tower Bridge; White Tower of the Tower of London.

Page 24 Left coin: Belgium (King). Centre: Luxembourg

(Grand Duke). Right: Netherlands (Queen Beatrix).

Page 24 The yellow objects are Gouda CHEESES.

Page 33 The brown smoke is from Mount Etna, an active volcano, which you can find on the map.

Pages 38–39 The script reads across the two pages:
1 Australia;
2 Egypt;
3 Hong Kong;
4 United States;
5 Taiwan.

Page 39 The five countries which share the shoreline of the Caspian Sea are Russia, Kazakhstan, Turkmenistan, Iran and Azerbaijan.

Page 40 The 15 'new' countries formed at the break-up of the USSR are (from largest to smallest): Russia, Kazakhstan, Ukraine, Turkmenistan, Uzbekistan, Belarus, Kyrgyzstan, Tajikistan, Azerbaijan, Georgia, Lithuania, Latvia, Estonia, Moldova and Armenia.

Page 41 Khabarovsk is on the River Amur. Moskva (= *Moscow*) to Vladivostok.

Page 44 Clockwise (from the top right-hand corner): samosas, ground coriander, coriander leaves, cumin, pakoras, rice, poppadums, red chilli powder next to yellow turmeric powder, green okra (also called 'ladies fingers'), garlic and bay leaves.

Page 50 These decorations are lanterns, made out of paper.

Page 65 Australia, of course!

Page 68 The north shores of Lakes Superior, Huron, Erie and Ontario are in Canada, and the south shores are in the USA. Lake Michigan is entirely in the USA.

Page 69 El Salvador only has a coastline on the Pacific Ocean. Belize only has a coastline on the Caribbean Sea. (Honduras has a tiny coastline on the Pacific – look closely at the map!) One island has two countries on it: Haiti and the Dominican Republic.

Page 73 Seattle to Miami is 5445 kilometres; New Orleans to Chicago is 1488 kilometres.

Page 76 The Spanish words mean: Amarillo = Yellow; Colorado = Coloured;

El Paso = The pass; Los Angeles = The angels; San José = St Joseph; San Francisco = St Francis.

Page 81 Aruba and Curaçao are part of the Netherlands; Turks Is, Caicos I., Grand Cayman, Anguilla and Montserrat are owned by the UK. The islands of Guadeloupe and Martinique are both part of France. Some of the Virgin Islands belong to the UK, and some belong to the USA. The island of Hispaniola is shared by Haiti and the Dominican Republic.

QUIZ ANSWERS (on pages 90–91)

NAME THE COUNTRY
1 Norway (Europe)
2 Thailand (Asia)
3 Mozambique (Africa)
4 Mexico (Central America)
5 Chile (South America)

NAME THE ISLAND
1 Iceland
2 Crete (Greece)
3 Sicily (Italy)
4 Sumatra (Indonesia)
5 Sulawesi (Indonesia)
6 Cuba
7 Honshu (Japan)
8 Baffin Island (Canada)
9 Madagascar
10 North Island (New Zealand)

A MYSTERY MESSAGE
I was *hungry*, so I bought a large *turkey*, some *swedes* and a bottle of *port*. Finally, I ate an *ice-cream*. I enjoyed my *meal*, but afterwards I began to *bulge* and I got a bad *pain*. A man told me: 'Just eat *pineapples* and *egg* cooked in a *pan*. Tomorrow you can eat a *banana* and some *Brazil* nuts. It shouldn't *cost* you too much.' I said: 'You must be *mad*! I think I've got *malaria*. I'll have *to go* to a doctor quickly, otherwise I'll soon be *dead*.'
Happily, the doctor *cured* me, so I am still *alive* today!

GREAT RIVERS OF EUROPE
1 Danube; 2 Rhine;
3 Rhône; 4 Severn; 5 Tagus.

PLACES IN ASIA
Countries
Iran; China; Oman; Taiwan; Nepal.
Capital cities
Manila; Riyadh; Tashkent; Kabul; Colombo.

COLOUR QUIZ
1 Red (Red Sea/Red River)
2 Green (Greenland/Green Bay)
3 Black (Black Sea/Black Forest)
4 Yellow (Yellow Sea/Yellowstone River)
5 White (White Sea/White Nile)
6 Orange (Orange/Orange River)
7 Blue (Blue Nile/Blue Ridge)

STATES OF THE USA
1 Texas
2 Rhode Island
3 Minnesota
4 Florida
5 Washington
6 Maine
7 Michigan
8 Maryland
9 Wyoming and Colorado
10 Oklahoma
11 Michigan
12 New York
13 Utah
14 Louisiana
15 South Dakota
16 North Carolina
17 Utah, Colorado, Arizona and New Mexico
18 Four (California, Arizona, New Mexico and Texas)
19 Three (Washington, Oregon and California)
20 Five (Texas, Louisiana, Mississippi, Alabama and Florida)

OCEANS AND SEAS
1 Pacific; 2 Atlantic;
3 Arctic; 4 Indian;
5 Atlantic;
6 Red Sea;
7 Sea of Japan;
8 North Sea;
9 South China Sea;
10 Caribbean Sea.

AFGHANISTAN	ALBANIA	ALGERIA	ANDORRA	ANGOLA	ANTIGUA & BARBUDA	ARGENTINA
BARBADOS	BELARUS	BELGIUM	BELIZE	BENIN	BHUTAN	BOLIVIA
CABO VERDE	CAMBODIA	CAMEROON	CANADA	CENTRAL AFRICAN REP.	CHAD	CHILE
CROATIA	CUBA	CYPRUS	CZECHIA	DENMARK	DJIBOUTI	DOMINICA
ESWATINI	ETHIOPIA	FIJI ISLANDS	FINLAND	FRANCE	GABON	GAMBIA
GUINEA	GUINEA-BISSAU	GUYANA	HAITI	HONDURAS	HUNGARY	ICELAND
JAMAICA	JAPAN	JORDAN	KAZAKHSTAN	KENYA	KIRIBATI	KOREA, NORTH
LESOTHO	LIBERIA	LIBYA	LIECHTENSTEIN	LITHUANIA	LUXEMBOURG	MACEDONIA
MAURITANIA	MAURITIUS	MEXICO	MICRONESIA	MOLDOVA	MONGOLIA	MONTENEGRO
NEW ZEALAND	NICARAGUA	NIGER	NIGERIA	NORTHERN MARIANAS	NORWAY	OMAN
PORTUGAL	PUERTO RICO	QATAR	ROMANIA	RUSSIA	RWANDA	SAMOA
SLOVAKIA	SLOVENIA	SOLOMON ISLANDS	SOMALIA	SOUTH AFRICA	SPAIN	SRI LANKA
SWITZERLAND	SYRIA	TAIWAN	TAJIKISTAN	TANZANIA	THAILAND	TIMOR-LESTE
UGANDA	UKRAINE	UNITED ARAB EMIRATES	UNITED KINGDOM	UNITED STATES	URUGUAY	UZBEKISTAN